*F*lying *C*olours

Students' Book **1**

Judy Garton-Sprenger   **Simon Greenall**

Heinemann

Heinemann International
A division of Heinemann Publishers (Oxford) Ltd
Halley Court, Jordan Hill, Oxford OX2 8EJ

OXFORD LONDON EDINBURGH MADRID PARIS ATHENS
BOLOGNA MELBOURNE SYDNEY AUCKLAND SINGAPORE
TOKYO IBADAN NAIROBI GABORONE HARARE
PORTSMOUTH (NH)

ISBN 0 435 28300 6

Cover illustration by Lo Cole
Illustrations by Olivia Bown, Colin Clifton, Lo Cole,
John Davey, Steve Fricker, John Gilkes, Val Hill,
David Mitcheson, Trevor Ridley, Jonathan Satchell,
Laurence Zeegan
Commissioned photographs by Paul Freestone, Chris
Honeywell

Typeset in 11/13 Garamond Original Roman by
Tradespools Ltd, Frome, Somerset
Printed in Scotland by Cambus Litho Ltd

94 95 10 9 8 7 6

ACKNOWLEDGMENTS

Many people have been involved in the creation, design and production of this book. The authors would particularly like to thank the editor, Liz Driscoll, for her contribution.

The authors and publishers would also like to thank the following teachers and their students who piloted the material: Rosylin Adams, (Instituto británico, Seville), Jane Arda (International House, London), Nick Dunn (Stanton School of English, Alicante), Isabel Duran (I.F.P. San Roque, Madrid), Peter Greaves (Casa Inglesa, Madrid), Kay Hodgson (Metropolis School of English, Granada), David Killick (St Giles College, Brighton), Simon White (Stanton School of English, Madrid). They would also like to thank the many teachers around the world who have helped develop the ideas in this book, in particular the participants on the British Council Nottingham Summer School.

Thanks are also due to James W. Richardson for producing the cassettes and the following people for their help with the authentic recordings: Celina Andrade Bicudo, Anna de Haas, Ellen Morgan, Marie-Louise Orler, Yassin Tabet, Timothy Walker, Sonja Zilsperger.

While every effort has been made to trace the owners of copyright material in this book, there have been some cases when the publishers have been unable to contact the owners. We should be grateful to hear from anyone who recognises their copyright material and who is unacknowledged. We shall be pleased to make the necessary amendments in future editions of the book.

The authors and publishers are grateful to the following for permission to reproduce copyright photographs: Ace Photo Library (photo: Paul H. Henning) p 25 (E); Adams Picture Library p 25 (C); Michael Boyd p 40 (mt, bl, br); Cheek by Jowl Theatre Company p 58; Christine Osborne Pictures/MEP p 48 (C); Cultural Co-operation (photo: Prakash Daswani) p 42 (International Festival of Street Music); English Life Publications Ltd p 40 (tr); Judy Garton-Sprenger pp 2–3 (signs); Illustrated London News Picture Library/Thomas Cook Collection p 63; John Hillelson Agency Ltd (photo: Bossu/Sygma p 4 (A), (photo: Laffont/Sygma) p 4 (D); Rob Judges p 103 (mr); The Kobal Collection (photo from 'Perfect', Columbia Pictures) p 79 (tr), p 78 (tl, br), p 79 (br); Ellen Morgan p 31 (1); The National Trust Photographic Library (photo: Mike Williams) p 40 (mb); New Shakespeare Company/Open Air Theatre (photo: Alastair Muir) pp 42–3 (Open Air production of A Midsummer Night's Dream); Redferns pp 2–3 (rock concert); p 83 (bl); Rex Features pp 8–9; Robert Harding Picture Library p 4 (C), p 11 (tl, tr), p 27 (ml, bl), p 30 (bl), p 39 (r, cr), p 40 (tr), p 49 (t, b), p 56 (t, m), p 57 (C), p 77, p 100; Roland Grant Archive (still from 'Cry Freedom', Universal Pictures) pp 42–3, (still from 'Once is Not Enough', Paramount Pictures) p 78 (bl), (still from 'Wall Street', 20th Century Fox) p 78 (tr); Sally and Richard Greenhill pp 2–3 (hotel sign), pp 4–5 (B), p 48 (D), p 80 (A, B, D); Singapore Airlines p 30 (tr); Syndication International p 64; Tony Stone Photo Library (photo: Mike Surowiak) p 24 (A), (photo: Thierry Cazabon) p 30 (tl), (photo: DGI.H) p 39 (1), (photo: David H. Endersbee) p 56 (br), (photo: A.P. Heaps) p 57 (A), (photo: Robert Everts) p 57 (D), (photo: Ian O'Leary) p 74, (photo: Jon Gray) p 75, (photo: Jon Riley) p 80 (C); Topham Picture Library p 30 (m, br), p 48 (A), p 57 (B), p 60, p 65, p 83 (tl, mt, tr, br); Virgin Atlantic Airways Ltd p 48 (B); Woodmansterne p 56 (1); Zefa p 31 (r), pp 42–3 (photo of gallery).

The authors and publishers are also grateful to the following for their kind permission to use copyright material in this book: pp 2–3 Levi Strauss & Co (jeans label); pp 6–7 Margaret Tarner (extract from Rebecca, by Daphne du Maurier, Heinemann Guided Readers Series, 1977), William Collins Sons & Co Ltd (extract from Cobuild English Language Dictionary, 1987), British Railways (timetable), J. Sainsbury (Gazpacho label), Century Hutchinson Ltd (for the poem 'Neighbours' by Sarah Smith from Cadbury's Fifth Book of Children's Poetry [Beaver Books, 1987]), Pan Books (extract from The Tropical Traveller by John Hatt (Pan Books, 1982); p 12 The Independent (for the articles 'Ivory Ban' and 'Bubbly Blighted' [12.5.1989], 'Deep Cheap Heat' and 'Temples Shifted' [17.5.1989], 'Mudslides' [20.5.1989] and 'English Draw' [24.5.1989]), The Observer (for articles 'Launch Delay' and 'Jet Hijack' [18.5.1989]); p 24 The Guardian (for 'Inky' cartoon by Ed McHenry [27.5.1987]); p 58 Cheek by Jowl Theatre Company (for use of their logo); p 60 Observer Magazine (for extracts from 'Case Histories' by Penny Rich [5.1.1986]); p 62 Penguin Books Inc (for cover of Beyond the Blue Horizon by Alexander Frater [Penguin Books, 1987]); p 67 Virago Press (for cover of West with the Night by Beryl Markham [Virago Press, 1989]); p 82 (entries from The Guinness Book of Records) copyright © Guinness Publishing Ltd, 1988; p 84 YOU Magazine Solo Syndication (for the profile of Adragon Demello from 'The World's Youngest Brain Boxes', [The Mail on Sunday, 11.9.1988]); pp 96–7 Ken Gibbs, Channel Tunnel Project, British Railways Board (for assistance in preparation of Channel Tunnel material); p 110, p 112 Simon and Schuster International Group (texts adapted from the Macdonald Countries Series).

CONTENTS

COMMUNICATIVE AIMS	STRUCTURES	TOPICS

*E*nglish
Everywhere 1

How much English do you know?
Saying it without words: Greetings round the world
What do we read? Different ways with words
Famous families: The Kennedys
Britain in view: Who lives in Britain?
PLUS
Down to business - Reading the cards

Hello!
and welcome to:

❶ Look at the photos. Find the international words.

❷ 📼 Listen and read.

bar   cinema   club   coffee   English   football   hamburger   hotel
jeans   pizza   restaurant   rock   sandwich   taxi   tennis   video

❸ 📼 Listen to four conversations. Tick (√) the words in activity 2 that you hear.

Say the other words in activity 2.

Now say five more international words.

❹ 📼 Listen and read.

Alphabet
A B C D E F G H I J K L M N O P Q R S T U V W X Y Z
a b c d e f g h i j k l m n o p q r s t u v w x y z

❺ 📼 Listen and write.

/eɪ/   /iː/   /ɛ/   /aɪ/   /juː/   /əʊ//ɑː/

A _ _ _   B _ _ _ _ _ _   F _ _ _ _ _ _ _ _   I _   Q _ _ _ _ _

Now say the letters.

❻ Spell your name.

Ramon Torres – R–A–M–O–N
T–O–double R–E–S

❼ 📼 Listen and read.

SYLVIE   Hello. What's your name?

MATTEO   Matteo, M–A–double T–E–O. What's your name?

SYLVIE   Sylvie, S–Y–L–V–I–E.

MATTEO   Thank you, Sylvie.

❽ 📼 Listen and repeat.

<u>name</u>   What's your <u>name</u>?
Hel<u>lo</u>.   What's your <u>name</u>?

❾ Ask and write names.

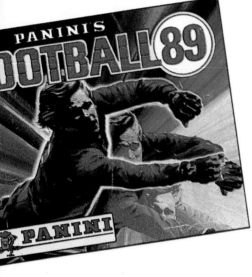

⑩ 📼 Listen and read the numbers.

1 one	4 four	7 seven	10 ten
2 two	5 five	8 eight	11 eleven
3 three	6 six	9 nine	12 twelve

Now say them aloud.

⑪ 📼 Listen and write numbers. Begin like this: 10

⑫ 📼 Listen and read.

⑬ 📼 Listen and number the words in activity 12.

⑭ Match the words with the pictures. What do the people mean?

Yes.   No.   Goodbye.   I don't understand.

📼 Listen and check.

⑮ Find eight words you know and eight new words.

> In this lesson you practise:
> • **Asking who people are**
> • **Spelling**
> Now turn to page 14 and look at the STRUCTURES TO LEARN **and the** WORDS TO REMEMBER.

❶ Say which places are countries and which are towns.

Britain   Naples   Tokyo
Italy   London   Germany
the Soviet Union   Spain
Paris   China   Rio   Australia
Japan   Greece   New York
Brazil   Canada   Athens
the United States of America
Argentina   Moscow   India
Switzerland   France

▭ **Now listen and check.
Repeat the place names.**

**❷ ▭ Listen to the news reports.
Tick the places you hear.**

❸ ▭ Listen and repeat.

A Where's Tokyo?
B It's in Japan.

❹ Ask and say where these places are.

Brasilia   Buenos Aires
Madras   Canberra   Milan
Geneva   Canton
Manchester   Bonn   Toronto
Kyoto   Piraeus   Leningrad
Granada   Dallas

❺ Read and match.

Canada   China   Britain
the Soviet Union   Japan   (Italy)

/brɪtən/   /kænədə/
/dʒəpæn/   /ɪtəli/   /tʃaɪnə/
/ðə səʊviət juːnjən/

**Now find words in this lesson
which begin with these sounds.**

/b/   /g/   /dʒ/   /k/   /m/
/p/   /s/   /t/

**Find words in this lesson which
end with these sounds.**

/ə/   /i/   /əʊ/

**❻ Say where the people in the photos are from. Choose from the
countries in activity 5.**

Photo A: the Soviet Union

SAYING IT W

WOR

⑦ Complete the conversation with these sentences.

a Where's that?
b Where are you from, Pierre?
c I'm from Italy.

SUZANNA ....
PIERRE   I'm from Quebec.
SUZANNA ....
PIERRE   It's in Canada. Where are you from?
SUZANNA ....

▭▭ **Now listen and check.**

⑧ Ask other students where they are from.

⑨ ▭▭ **Listen and number the greetings as you hear them.**

Good morning.
`0900`

Good afternoon.
`1500`

Good evening.
`2200`

Now greet other students.

⑩ ▭▭ **Listen and read the numbers.**

| 13 thirteen | 15 fifteen | 17 seventeen | 19 nineteen |
| 14 fourteen | 16 sixteen | 18 eighteen | 20 twenty |

⑪ Work in pairs

STUDENT A   **Say a number.**
STUDENT B   **Point at the number you hear.**

3   12   7   20   18   4   2   11   9   16   5   8

⑫ Find these words in this lesson.

China   3
America   1
Britain   2

number

✓

tick

Bon n

find

④ —— four

match

the Soviet U n i o n

complete

point

▭▭ **Now listen and number the words.**

⑬ These words from other languages are used in English. Are they used in your language? What do they mean?

café   sushi   pasta   macho   ballet   salon   sauerkraut   samba
macaroni   alpha   sauna   karate   boutique   samurai   chili   drama

Are any more words from your language used in English?

> **In this lesson you practise:**
> ● **Greeting people**
> ● **Asking and saying where people are from**
> ● **Asking and saying where places are**
> ● **Prepositions of place : *in, from***
> Now turn to page 15 and look at the STRUCTURES TO LEARN and the WORDS TO REMEMBER.

❶ Say which things you read in your language.

newspapers   novels   labels
magazines   brochures
timetables   reference books
letters   English textbooks
notices and signs

Tick the things you can find in English.

Now say what you want to read in English.

❷ Look at WHAT DO WE READ? Circle the words you recognise.

Now say where the extracts are from. Choose from the words in activity 1.

❸ Look at the job advertisements and find six jobs.

📼 **Now listen and match the jobs with the pictures.**

❹ Find out the English word for your job.

Now ask and say.

A   What do you do? / What's your job?

B   I'm a/an (job). / I'm a student.

What do we

Without a word, he started the
tears began to run dow
my hand

30 Jackson Road,
London N7 6EJ

21 May 1989

Dear Carol,
Here's your theatre ticket
for Tuesday evening. The
...s at 8 p.m, and
...g Simon and Jill
...g next to the

Tw
and
bags
emp
M
brea
child
woul
Th
Wint
on m
'W
can't
arlo
'I'v
'We
're
ryt
be

RECEPTIONIST for lunch time relief required for prestigious offices in Victoria. Call O.V. Selection. (Rec. Cons).

SECRETARY Solicitors EC4 S/hand Manual Typewriter Gd Sal 4 days PW. Phone 726 1432

SHOP ASSISTANT working with young people Camden area. Hours negotiable. Telephone 482 2736

ENGINEER London & Home Counties. Immediate start. Call 0714 313629

ACCOUNTANT required by busy expanding contract company based in Putney, must be fully experienced. Good salary and fringe benefits. Salary review after short period. Reply Box no 241

EFL TEACHER Established language centre in Madrid requires Teacher for October. Must have RSA Cert. or Dip., and experience. We offer good working conditions, salary and opportunities for professional development. Interviews in London, mid June. Please send curriculum vitae and references to:

SAINSBURY

Gourmet So

GAZPACH

SPANISH STYLE CUCUM
AND TOMATO SOU

ALUES
PER HALF
AN SERVING
0 k CALORIES
0 k. JOULES
7 g
7 g
g

Thursday /ˈθɜːzdɪ¹/, **Thursdays**. Thursday is one of the seven days of the week. It is the day after Wednesday and before Friday. EG I got your postcard on Thursday... The question was raised at the meeting last Thursday.

thus /ðʌs/; a fairly formal word. I You use thus to show that what you are about to mention is the result or consequence of something else that you have jus mentioned. EG ...former miners who are now down t ...ir last 2,000 pounds and thus qualify for socia

5 Look at these words. What are they? Find them in WHAT DO WE READ?

Monday Tuesday Wednesday Thursday Friday Saturday Sunday

Now match the words with their sounds.

/θɜːzdeɪ/ /sʌndeɪ/ /tjuːzdeɪ/ /sætədeɪ/ /wɛnzdeɪ/ /mʌndeɪ/ /fraɪdeɪ/

▦ Now listen and repeat.

6 Find words in this lesson which begin with these sounds.

/f/ /d/ /l/ /n/ /r/ /θ/ /ð/ /w/

Find five words in this lesson which contain the sound /s/ and five words which contain the sound /z/.

7 ▦ Listen and tick the words you hear.

/ʃɒp/ /njuːspeɪpə/ /bʊk/ /tiːtʃə/ /sɜkrətri/ /lɛtə/
/əkaʊntənt/ /mægəziːn/ /stjuːdənt/ /dʒɒb/

8 Find these words in this lesson.

word picture activity lesson phrase sound

▦ Now listen and number the words in the order you hear them.

9 Read.

The most useful words

John Hatt, author of 'The Tropical Traveller', has visited more than fifty countries. When he goes to a foreign country, he learns this list of words and phrases in the foreign language:

please thank you tea how much? too much where (is)? good/beautiful bad/ugly I do not speak (Arabic) (I am) British (what is the) name (of this)? (is that) safe? sorry hello yes no

Find out what the words and phrases mean. When can you use them?

What does 'too much' mean?

10 Choose ten English words and phrases that are useful to you.

> In this lesson you practise:
> ● Asking and saying what people do
> ● Articles: *a* and *an*
> Now turn to page 16 and look at the STRUCTURES TO LEARN and the WORDS TO REMEMBER.

FOUR

VE MONTE CARLO

ything had changed. Mrs Van Hopper
eave Monte Carlo. All the trunks and
All the drawers and cupboards were

ad read the letter from her daughter at
ailing for New York on Saturday. Her
ing too. I'm tired of living here. How
New York?'

aving Monte Carlo and Maxim de
one. My unhappiness must have shown

ld you are,'
. I though

I said.
o get use
e boat as
o down t
unhapp
ntly at

Flight of fantasy...

A FRENCHMAN who intended to fly from Paris to Manchester, Massachusetts, ended up in Manchester, England, 3,500 miles adrift, after boarding the wrong plane.

INTERCITY

oventry → London

al train service 3 October 1988 to 14 May 1989

days to Saturdays		Sundays		
Coventry depart	London Euston arrive		Coventry depart	London Euston arrive
0611 SK	0732	B IC	0823 n	1047
0640	0800	A IC	0840	1029
0710 SK	0827	C IC	0841	1047
0740 SK	3857	B IC	0923 n	1147
0740 SO	0900	A IC	0940	1129
0810 SO	0921	C IC	0941	1147
0810 SO	0924	B IC	1023 n	1242
0840	0951	A IC	1040	1225
0910	1026	C IC	1041	1242
0930	1056 k	A IC	1100	1243
0940	1057	B IC	1103 n	1323
1010	1129	B IC	1120 n	1343
1040 SK	1205	C IC	1121	1323
1110	1233	A IC	1140	1326
1140 SK	1304	C IC	1141	1343
1210	1331	B IC	1223 n	1443
1240 SK	1359	A IC	1240	1426
1310	1434	C IC	1241	1443
1340 SO	1459	B IC	1323 n	1541
1340 SK	1503	A IC	1340	1525
1410 SK	1535	C IC	1341	1541
1440	1559	A IC	1403 n	1627
1510	1635	A IC	1420	1614
1540 SK	1659	C IC	1421	1619
1610	1724	B IC	1423 n	1638
1630 fo	1744	A IC	1440	1624
1640 SK	1755	C IC	1441	1624
1710 SO	1825	B IC	1453 n	1713
1710 SK	1828	A C IC	1510	1700

❶ Where can you listen to English in your town? Read and tick the chart.

Where can you listen to English?

- ☐ at the airport
- ☐ in films at the cinema
- ☐ at English-speaking theatres
- ☐ with teachers of English
- ☐ with tourists and guides
- ☐ with family and friends
- ☐ with au pairs
- ☐ at hotels and youth hostels
- ☐ at the embassy and consulate
- ☐ on the radio
- ☐ in films on TV and video
- ☐ at English language clubs
- ☐ at school
- ☐ in pop songs
- ☐ at church
- ☐ at English pubs
- ☐ with students
- ☐ at sports meetings

❷ 📼 Listen to three situations and answer the questions.

1 How many people can you hear?
2 Are they men or women?
3 Where are they?

❸ 📼 Listen again and number the words.

Venice   number   Handel   morning   seven   London   afternoon   house

Now match the words with the sounds.

/hændəl/   /ɑːftənuːn/   /vɛnɪs/   /haʊs/   /lʌndən/   /nʌmbə/ /sɛvən/   /mɔːnɪŋ/

❹ Say these words.

/sɪnəmə/   /θɪətə/   /ɪŋglɪʃ/   /tiːtʃə/   /hɒstəl/   /skuːl/ /klʌb/   /vɪdɪəʊ/

Find other words in this lesson which contain these sounds.

/h/   /tʃ/   /ɒ/   /ʌ/   /v/

❺ 📼 Look at FAMOUS FAMILIES – THE KENNEDYS. Listen and complete the family tree. Use these words.

mother   wife   aunt   sister   cousin

FAMOUS FAMILIES

THE KEN

In 1960, Jack Kennedy became President of the USA. In 1984, Joe Kennedy became Congressman for the State of

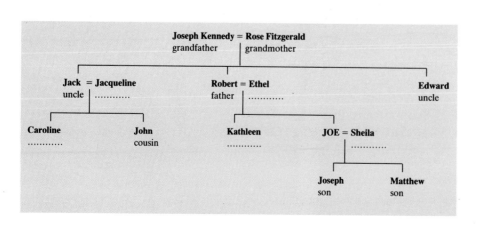

Joseph Kennedy = Rose Fitzgerald
grandfather   grandmother

Jack = Jacqueline
uncle   ....

Robert = Ethel
father   ....

Edward
uncle

Caroline
....

John
cousin

Kathleen
....

JOE = Sheila
....

Joseph
son

Matthew
son

❻ Complete the list.

wife	*husband*
mother	....
daughter	....
sister	....
aunt	....
niece	....
grandmother	....
granddaughter	....

JEDYS

Massachusetts. He's Jack
Kennedy's nephew, and Robert
Kennedy's son. Will Joe
become President?

8 ☰ **Listen and complete the chart for Ramon and Mireille.**

	Maria	Ramon	Mireille
married	*yes*		
children	*no*		
brothers/sisters	*2 brothers* *1 sister*		

9 ☰ **Listen and repeat the questions in activity 7.**

Now ask three students about their families.

10 ☰ **Listen to two conversations. Tick the words you hear.**

brother	→	brothers
sister		sisters
boy		boys
girl		girls

child	→	children
family		families
man		men
woman		women

Listen again and write the numbers you hear.

11 ☰ **Listen and repeat the numbers.**

21 twenty-one	40 forty	70 seventy	100 a hundred
22 twenty-two	50 fifty	80 eighty	
30 thirty	60 sixty	90 ninety	

12 **Match the numbers with the words.**

48   25   83   (72)   69   31   56   94

(seventy-two)   ninety-four   twenty-five   thirty-one
forty-eight   fifty-six   sixty-nine   eighty-three

13 ☰ **Listen to the conversations. Tick the numbers you hear.**

| **a** 16   60 | **c** 17   70 | **e** 18   80 |
| **b** 19   90 | **d** 13   30 | **f** 15   50 |

14 **Look at the clocks. Say the times.**

7 ☰ **Listen and read.**

INTERVIEWER   What's your name?
MARIA   Maria.
INTERVIEWER   Are you married?
MARIA   Yes.
INTERVIEWER   Have you got any children?
MARIA   No.
INTERVIEWER   Have you got any brothers and sisters?
MARIA   Yes. I've got two brothers and a sister.

In this lesson you practise:
● **Asking for and giving personal details (1)**
● **Plurals of nouns**
Now turn to page 17 and look at the STRUCTURES TO LEARN and the WORDS TO REMEMBER.

❶ Say which things you write in your language.

letters to friends   business letters   stories   diaries   messages   poems
reports   articles   exam essays   information on forms   lecture notes

Now say which things you want to write in English.

❷ Say what these documents are. Choose from the words in activity 1.

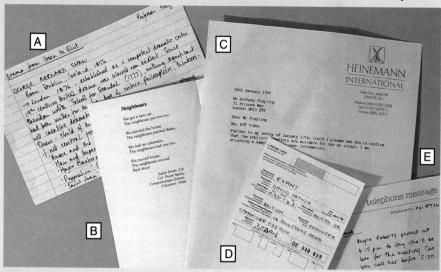

❸ Match the countries with the nationalities.

France   Greece   Spain   Poland   Germany   Portugal   China
Italy   Britain   Japan

Italian   British   French   Chinese   Spanish   Greek   German
Portuguese   Japanese   Polish

▭ **Now listen and repeat.**

❹ Find out the nationality of people from these places.

Australia   Brazil   Mexico   Peru   the United States   Canada
Switzerland   Hong Kong

What languages do they speak? Choose from these words.

Spanish   English   French   German   Italian   Chinese   Portuguese

❺ Say what nationality you are. What language(s) do you speak?

I'm <u>British</u>. I speak <u>English</u> and <u>French</u>.

❻ Say these words.

/ɪŋglənd/   /dʒəpæn/   /dʒɜːməni/   /pɔːtjʊgəl/   /ɒstreɪlɪə/
/ɪŋglɪʃ/   /dʒæpəniːz/   /dʒɜːmən/   /pɔːtjʊgiːz/   /ɒstreɪlɪən/

❼ ▭ Listen to the sports commentary. Tick the words in activity 6 that you hear.

Now find other words in this lesson which contain these sounds.

/ŋ/   /ʃ/   /æ/   /ɜː/   /ɔː/   /eɪ/

❽ Look at the BRITAIN IN VIEW photos. What nationality do you think the people are?

Now read and find out.

Jasmin Patel

❾ Read the clues and find out about the people in the BRITAIN IN VIEW photos.

1 How old are they?
2 What do they do?
3 Where do they live? Choose from the towns on the map.

Complete the chart on the right.

Clues
1   Jasmin Patel is a doctor.
2   Martha Chu is 19.
3   The secretary is 20 and she lives in London.
4   Louis Seaga lives in Scotland.
5   Martin Clark is an accountant.
6   The waiter is 31 and he lives in Wales.
7   The 37-year-old woman lives in Leeds.
8   The student lives in Manchester.
9   The engineer is 26.
10   The man who lives in Ireland is 43.

Britain in view

Who lives in Britain? The English, the Scottish, the Welsh and the Northern Irish. But is that all? In fact, people from all over the world live in Britain, and many of them are British now.

Who lives in Britain?

Martha Chu

SCOTLAND

● Edinburgh

NORTHERN IRELAND

Belfast ●

Leeds ●

● Manchester

WALES   ENGLAND

Cardiff ●

● London

Stavros Tavridis

Louis Seaga

Jean Slater

Martin Clark

All these people are British.

⑩ 📼 Listen to the addresses and say who is speaking. Choose from the people in the BRITAIN IN VIEW photos.

Now listen again and write the numbers you hear.

⑪ Ask and write addresses and phone numbers.

What's your ad<u>dress</u>?
What's your <u>phone</u> number?

⑫ Talk about the people in your country. What nationalities are they?

In this lesson you practise:
● Asking for and giving personal details (2)
Now turn to page 18 and look at the STRUCTURES TO LEARN and the WORDS TO REMEMBER.

name	age	job	town
Jasmin Patel		*doctor*	
Stavros Tavridis			
Martha Chu			
Louis Seaga			
Jean Slater			
Martin Clark			

❶ Read the radio news headlines.

a **An eleven-year-old boy takes off to fly round the world.**
b **Boris Becker wins after a hurricane stops the match.**
c **The Prime Minister returns from the Far East.**
d **Robbers steal £50,000 from a London bank.**
e **A train crashes at 180 km/h and no one is hurt.**
f **A Russian teacher finds his sister after fifty years.**

Match two words from the list below with each news item.

family police pilot hospital plane tennis Japan brother
tour game passengers money

❷ ▭ Listen to the news and number the headlines in activity 1.

Listen again and tick the words as you hear them.

❸ Read the newspaper items and circle any words you recognise.

Ivory ban

Nairobi (AFP) – Kenya wants a total worldwide ban on the ivory trade in a bid to stop elephant poaching, the Minister for Tourism, Katana Ngala, said. Between 200 and 300 elephants have been slaughtered so far this year by poachers in Kenya, officials say.

Temples shifted

New Delhi (AFP) – Indian engineers have transplanted a cluster of 20 ancient temples to a new site, to save them from being submerged by a dam, in a rare archaeological feat that took 10 years to accomplish.

Bubbly blighted

Paris (AP) – A spring frost that hit vines in eastern France will mean fewer bottles of bubbly in 1989, the Champagne producers association said.

Tunnel blaze

Bolzano (Reuter) – Two people were killed and four seriously injured when fire broke out in the main Brenner Pass motorway tunnel between Italy and Austria during maintenance work. The tunnel was closed and the victims are all thought to be Italian workers.

Deep cheap heat

Reykjavik (Reuter) – Iceland, which has vast reserves of unused hydro and geothermal power, hopes to sell cheap electricity to Britain through a 594-mile undersea cable.

Mudslides kill 50

Sao Paulo (Reuter) – More than 50 people are feared dead in mudslides which smashed through shantytowns in Brazil's north-eastern city of Salvador after torrential rain, authorities said. Some 2,500 people were made homeless.

England draw

England drew 0-0 with Chile before a crowd of 15,628, their lowest for a Wembley international. Liverpool beat West Ham 5-1 to relegate them to the Second Division.

LAUNCH DELAY

The long-delayed launch in French Guiana of Ariane-4, the European Space Agency's biggest rocket, was postponed again for at least several days because of problems with its fuel supply.

JET HIJACK

An American Airlines jet carrying 157 people from Dallas to Miami was hijacked by a man demanding to be flown to Havana, but landed safely in Miami, where police surrounded it.

Julie Duncan
EFL Teacher
Via Maiocchi 17
20129 Milano
(02) 22 66 24

READING
THE CARDS

❹ Complete the dialogue with these sentences.

a I think it's in Morocco.
b I don't know.
c It's in Peru.
d Is it in Algeria?

MARK Where's Lima?
LINDA ....
MARK That's right. Where's Oran?
LINDA ....
MARK No, it isn't.
LINDA ....
MARK Yes, it is. Where's Mana
LINDA ....
MARK It's in Brazil.

▭ Listen and check.

❺ Ask and say where these places a

Sarajevo Amsterdam Calgary
Bilbao Osaka Antwerp
Montevideo Houston Nairob

❻ Work in pairs. When you hear the numbers on the left, say the numbers on the right.

STUDENT A fifty-nine
STUDENT B thirty-five

STUDENT A		STUDENT B	
hear	say	hear	say
24	59	77	42
63	80	18	63
42	93	59	35
51	18	93	51
35	77	80	24

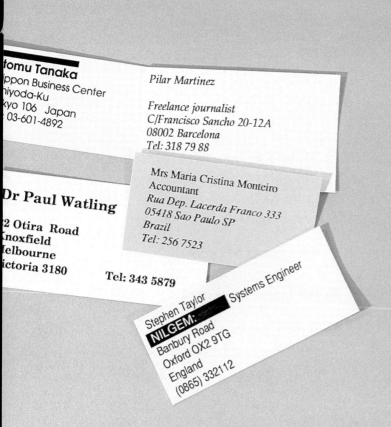

Tomu Tanaka
Nippon Business Center
Chiyoda-Ku
Tokyo 106   Japan
03-601-4892

Pilar Martinez

Freelance journalist
C/Francisco Sancho 20-12A
08002 Barcelona
Tel: 318 79 88

Mrs Maria Cristina Monteiro
Accountant
Rua Dep. Lacerda Franco 333
05418 Sao Paulo SP
Brazil
Tel: 256 7523

Dr Paul Watling

2 Otira Road
Knoxfield
Melbourne
Victoria 3180

Tel: 343 5879

Stephen Taylor   Systems Engineer
NILGEM
Banbury Road
Oxford OX2 9TG
England
(0865) 332112

7 Look at the business cards and circle the jobs. What nationality are the people?

I think Stomu is Japanese.

8 Work in pairs. Ask and answer questions.

What's your name?
What do you do?/What's your job?
What's your address?
What's your phone number?

Now write a business card for your partner.

9 ▭ Listen to Helen and Jack, and find out who these people are.

Alice   Andrew   David   Jill   Peter   Sophie

Complete Helen's family tree.

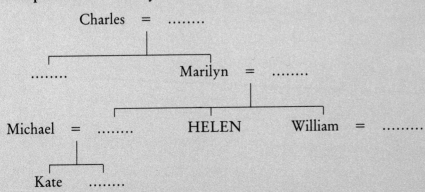

Charles   = ...

....   Marilyn   = ...

Michael   = ...   HELEN   William   = ...

Kate   ....

10 Look at Lessons 1–5. Choose:

- five words which you think are useful.
- five words which sound nice.
- five words which look like words in your language.
- five words which you often see in your country.

Write the words in your vocabulary notebook.

11 These words from other languages are used in English. What language are they?

fez spaghetti tortilla
delicatessen restaurant
delta concerto kebab
glasnost forum junta
samovar guerilla piano
rumba siesta graffiti
media cuisine bungalow
judo omelette kindergarten
mascara route

A I think 'fez' is a Russian word.
B No, I think it's Turkish.

12 Read these letters.

ANY QUESTIONS?

*WRITE TO THE
LANGUAGE
DOCTOR*

QUESTION   How do you say the number '0' in English?
Ana, Cadiz

ANSWER   In English, we say 0 in different ways:

oh

nil

zero

Have you got any questions about English? Write a letter to the language doctor and give it to your teacher.

STRUCTURES TO LEARN

Asking who people are
    What's your name?

See also *Lesson 6 LANGUAGE STUDY.*

WORDS TO REMEMBER

1 one /wʌn/   2 two /tu:/   3 three /θri:/
4 four /fɔ:/   5 five /faɪv/   6 six /sɪks/
7 seven /sɛvən/   8 eight /eɪt/   9 nine /naɪn/
10 ten /tɛn/   11 eleven /ɪlɛvən/
12 twelve /twɛlv/

ask /ɑ:sk/   listen /lɪsən/   read /ri:d/
repeat /rɪpi:t/   say /seɪ/   spell /spɛl/
write /raɪt/

name /neɪm/

yes /jɛs/   no /nəʊ/   hello /hələʊ/
goodbye /gʊdbaɪ/   thank you /θæŋk ju:/

a /eɪ/   b /bi:/   c /si:/   d /di:/   e /i:/   f /ɛf/
g /dʒi:/   h /eɪtʃ/   i /aɪ/   j /dʒeɪ/   k /keɪ/
l /ɛl/   m /ɛm/   n /ɛn/   o /əʊ/   p /pi:/
q /kju:/   r /ɑ:/   s /ɛs/   t /ti:/   u /ju:/   v /vi:/
w /dʌbəlju:/   x /ɛks/   y /waɪ/   z /zɛd/

PRACTICE EXERCISES

1 ▪▪ Listen and tick the numbers you hear.

Example: *seven*

1   2   3   4   5   6
7✓ 8   9   10   11   12

2 Write these numbers in order. Begin like this: *one, two*

three   ten   eight   one   six   eleven   nine
two   five   twelve   four   seven

▪▪ Listen and check the numbers.

3 ▪▪ Listen and write the numbers you hear.

4 Write these words in alphabetical order. Begin like this: *bar, eleven*

hello   football   restaurant   video   write
taxi   bar   rock   pizza   English   eleven
read   sandwich   tennis   seven

▪▪ Listen and number the words you hear.

5 ▪▪ Spell these words.

Example: *club*
            C–L–U–B

1 club
2 repeat
3 hamburger
4 goodbye
5 eight
6 spell

6 ▪▪ Ask and write names.

Example: *One*
            What's your name?
            Costas. C–O–S–T–A–S.
            Costas

STRUCTURES TO LEARN

Greeting people
Good morning.
Good afternoon.
Good evening.

Asking and saying where people are from
Where are you from?   I'm from Pisa.

Asking and saying where places are
Where's Pisa?   It's in Italy.

See also *Lessons 6 and 16 LANGUAGE STUDY.*

Prepositions of place: *in, from*
Julio Iglesias is *from* Spain. He's Spanish.
Diego Maradona is *from* Argentina. He's
Argentinian.

Madras is *in* India.
Geneva is *in* Switzerland.

For more prepositions of place, see *Lessons 13, 14*
and *16 LANGUAGE STUDY.*

WORDS TO REMEMBER

13 thirteen /θɜːtiːn/   14 fourteen /fɔːtiːn/
15 fifteen /fɪftiːn/   16 sixteen /sɪkstiːn/
17 seventeen /sɛvəntiːn/   18 eighteen /eɪtiːn/
19 nineteen /naɪntiːn/   20 twenty /twɛnti/

complete /kəmpliːt/   find /faɪnd/   match /mætʃ/
number /nʌmbə/   point /pɔɪnt/   tick /tɪk/

country /kʌntri/   place /pleɪs/   town /taʊn/

Argentina /ɑːdʒəntiːnə/   Australia /ɒstreɪliə/
Brazil /brəzɪl/   Britain /brɪtən/
Canada /kænədə/   China /tʃaɪnə/   France /frɑːns/
Germany /dʒɜːməni/   Greece /griːs/
India /ɪndiə/   Italy /ɪtəli/   Japan /dʒəpæn/
the Soviet Union /ðə səʊvɪət juːnjən/
Spain /speɪn/   Switzerland /swɪtsələnd/
the United States of America /ðə juːnaɪtɪd steɪts əv
əmɛrɪkə/

PRACTICE EXERCISES

❶ ▭ **Listen and tick the names you hear.**

Margaret Thatcher   Severiano Ballesteros
Pope John Paul   Giorgio Armani   Helmut Kohl
George Bush   Michael Jackson   Tina Turner
Diego Maradona   Mikhail Gorbachev

❷ **Find names in exercise 1 which begin with these
sounds.**
1 /b/   2 /dʒ/   3 /g/   4 /k/
5 /m/   6 /p/   7 /s/   8 /t/

▭ **Listen and check.**

❸ **Read and match the words with their sounds.**
1 /æθənz/   4 /neɪpəlz/   Naples   New York
2 /pærɪs/   5 /riːəʊ/   Rio   Moscow
3 /mɒskəʊ/   6 /njuː jɔːk/   Athens 1   Paris

▭ **Listen and check. Repeat the words.**

❹ ▭ **Now say where places are. Choose from this
list of countries.**

America   Greece   France   Italy
the Soviet Union   Brazil

Example: *Where's Athens?*
It's in Greece.

❺ ▭ **Ask where people are from. Listen and
number the places.**

Example: *One*
Where are you from?
I'm from Australia.

Tokyo   Australia 1   Argentina
New York   Brazil   Rio
Naples   Quebec   Italy
Moscow   Paris   Athens

❻ **Write** *in* **or** *from.*

1 Quebec is ... Canada.
2 Pope John Paul is ... Poland, but he's now ...
Rome.
3 New York is ... the United States of America.
4 The Italian designer Giorgio Armani is ... Milan.
5 – Where's Milan?
– It's ... Italy.
6 – Where are you ...?
– I'm ... London.

▭ **Listen and check.**

❼ ▭ **Say the next three numbers in the sequence.**

Example: *20   19   18   17   16*
15   14   13

20	19	18	17	16
1	3	5	7	9
2	4	6	8	10
20	18	16	14	12
1	2	4	5	7

STRUCTURES TO LEARN

Asking and saying what people do

What do you do? What's your job?	I'm a student. I'm a teacher. I'm an engineer.

See also *Lesson 8 LANGUAGE STUDY*.

Articles: *a* and *an*

The indefinite article is *a* or *an*. You use *a* /ə/ before a consonant and the sound /juː/.

a secretary
a word
a student
a university

You use *an* /ən/ before a vowel.

an accountant
an activity
an engineer

WORDS TO REMEMBER

Monday /mʌndeɪ/   Tuesday /tjuːzdeɪ/
Wednesday /wɛnzdeɪ/   Thursday /θɜːzdeɪ/
Friday /fraɪdeɪ/   Saturday /sætədeɪ/
Sunday /sʌndeɪ/

job /dʒɒb/   accountant /əkauntənt/
engineer /ɛndʒɪnɪə/   receptionist /rɪsɛpʃənɪst/
secretary /sɛkrətri/   shop assistant /ʃɒp əsɪstənt/
student /stjuːdənt/   teacher /tiːtʃə/

activity /æktɪvɪti/   lesson /lɛsən/   phrase /freɪz/
picture /pɪktʃə/   sound /saund/   word /wɜːd/

please /pliːz/   sorry /sɒri/

bad /bæd/   beautiful /bjuːtɪfʊl/   good /gʊd/
ugly /ʌgli/

PRACTICE EXERCISES

❶ Which words have two syllables? Which words have three syllables?

picture 2	magazine 3	engineer
Wednesday	Thursday	teacher
secretary	accountant	lesson
Friday	receptionist	label
newspaper	assistant	letter

▣ Now listen and check. Repeat the words.

❷ Find words in exercise 1 which begin with these sounds.

1 /f/   2 /l/   3 /n/   4 /r/   5 /s/   6 /θ/   7 /w/

▣ Now listen and check.

❸ Read the words in exercise 1 again and write a list of the jobs.

▣ Listen and check.

❹ ▣ Ask what people do. Listen and number the jobs in your list.

Example: *One*
        What do you do?
        I'm an accountant.

❺ Read and match the words with their sounds.

1 /gʊd/   please
2 /nəʊ/   thank you
3 /sɒri/   good
4 /jɛs/   sorry
5 /pliːz/   hello
6 /θæŋk juː/   yes
7 /hələʊ/   no

▣ Listen and check. Repeat the words.

❻ Write *a*, *an* or –.

1 – Where's . . . New York?
   – It's in . . . America.
2 – What do you do?
   – I'm . . . accountant.
3 – Where are you from?
   – I'm from . . . Montevideo.
4 I'm . . . student of English.
5 Jean Simmons is . . . receptionist from . . . Manchester.
6 How do you spell . . . engineer?

▣ Listen and check.

STRUCTURES TO LEARN

Asking for and giving personal details (1)

Are you married?	Yes./No.
Have you got any children?	Yes. I've got a/one son.
Have you got any brothers and sisters?	Yes. I've got two sisters.

See also *Lessons 5, 6 and 8 LANGUAGE STUDY*.

Plurals of nouns

You form the plural of most nouns with -s.

boy	boys
brother	brothers
girl	girls
sister	sisters

You add -ies to nouns ending in consonant -y.

country	countries
city	cities
family	families

You add -es to nouns ending in -ch, -ss, -sh, -x.

sandwich	sandwiches

Some nouns have irregular plurals.

child	children
wife	wives
man	men
woman	women

The plural of *person* is usually *people*.

WORDS TO REMEMBER

aunt /ɑ:nt/ boy /bɔɪ/ brother /brʌðə/
cousin /kʌzən/ daughter /dɔ:tə/ father /fɑ:ðə/
girl /gɜ:l/ granddaughter /grændɔ:tə/
grandfather /grændfɑ:ðə/
grandmother /grændmʌðə/
grandson /grændsʌn/ husband /hʌzbənd/
mother /mʌðə/ nephew /nɛfju:/ niece /ni:s/
sister /sɪstə/ son /sʌn/ uncle /ʌŋkəl/

child /tʃaɪld/ children /tʃɪldrən/
family /fæmɪli/ families /fæmɪlɪz/ man /mæn/
men /mɛn/ wife /waɪf/ wives /waɪvz/
woman /wʊmən/ women /wɪmɪn/

21 twenty-one /twɛnti wʌn/
22 twenty-two /twɛnti tu:/ 30 thirty /θɜ:ti/
40 forty /fɔ:ti/ 50 fifty /fɪfti/ 60 sixty /sɪksti/
70 seventy /sɛvənti/ 80 eighty /eɪti/
90 ninety /naɪnti/ 100 a hundred /ə hʌndrəd/

PRACTICE EXERCISES

1 Say these words.

/həʊtɛl/ /spɔ:t/ /pʌb/ /ɛəpɔ:t/ tʃɜ:tʃə/
/reɪdɪəʊ/ /pɒp sɒŋ/ /stju:dənt/

▬▬ Listen and check. Repeat the words.

2 ▬▬ Ask questions. Listen and complete the chart.

Example: *name*
    What's your name?
    Alan Gower

name	*Alan Gower*
married	
children	
brothers and sisters	

3 Match the numbers with the words.

29	forty-three
34	forty
36	seventy-five
40	twenty-nine
43	sixty-two
57	eighty-eight
62	thirty-six
75	ninety-one
88	fifty-seven
91	thirty-four

▬▬ Listen and tick the numbers you hear.

4 ▬▬ Ask the time. Listen and write the times.

Example: *One.*
    What's the time?
    It's one forty-five. 1.45

5 ▬▬ Now answer questions and say the times.

Example: *One.*
    What's the time?
    It's one forty-five.

6 Complete the sentences with the singular or plural form of the words in brackets.

1 Have you got any . . .? (child)
2 My . . . is an engineer. (mother)
3 There are three people in my . . . . (family)
4 I've got two . . . . (brother)
5 How many . . . are there in Africa? (country)
6 There are twenty . . . in my class. (student)

▬▬ Listen and check.

STRUCTURES TO LEARN

Asking for and giving personal details (2)
What's your address?
What's your phone number?

I'm Portuguese.
I speak French and Italian.

See also *Lessons 4, 6* and *8 LANGUAGE STUDY.*

WORDS TO REMEMBER

England /ɪŋlənd/   Mexico /mɛksɪkəʊ/
Peru /pəru:/   Poland /pəʊlənd/
Portugal /pɔ:tjʊgəl/

American /əmɛrɪkən/   Australian /ɒstreɪlɪən/
Brazilian /brəzɪlɪən/   British /brɪtɪʃ/
Canadian /kəneɪdɪən/   Chinese /tʃaɪni:z/
English /ɪŋlɪʃ/   French /frɛntʃ/
German /dʒɜ:mən/   Greek /gri:k/
Italian /ɪtæljən/   Japanese /dʒæpəni:z/
Mexican /mɛksɪkən/   Peruvian /pəru:vɪən/
Polish /pəʊlɪʃ/   Portuguese /pɔ:tjʊgi:z/
Spanish /spænɪʃ/   Swiss /swɪs/

doctor /dɒktə/   waiter /weɪtə/   waitress /weɪtrəs/

live /lɪv/   speak /spi:k/

address /ədrɛs/   language /læŋgwɪdʒ/
nationality /næʃənælɪti/
phone number /fəʊn nʌmbə/

PRACTICE EXERCISES

① **Match countries with nationalities.**

France   Italian
China   British
Italy   Spanish
Britain   Greek
Portugal   German
Greece   French
Spain   Chinese
Germany   Portuguese

▣ **Say what nationality people are.**

Example: *He's from France.*
He's French.

② **Find words in exercise 1 which contain these sounds.**

1 /ʃ/   2 /æ/   3 /eɪ/   4 /ɜ:/   5 /ɔ:/

▣ **Listen and check. Repeat the words.**

③ **Write the country or nationality.**

1 Julio Iglesias is . . . . (Spain/Spanish)
2 The name *Mireille* is . . . . (France/French)
3 The English, Welsh, Northern Irish and Scottish
   are all . . . . (Britain/British)
4 – Where are you from?
   – I'm from . . . . (Italy/Italian)
5 I speak a little . . . .(Portugal/Portuguese)

▣ **Listen and check.**

④ **Complete the dialogue.**

A Hello, what's . . . name?
B Martin.
A And where . . . you from?
B I'm . . . Belfast.
A And what . . . you do?
B . . . an accountant.

Underline the important words.

▣ **Listen and check.**

⑤ ▣ **Listen to the questions in exercise 4 and talk about yourself.**

⑥ ▣ **Ask people their addresses. Listen and correct the information.**

Example: *One*
What's your address?
14 London Road, Southampton

1 40 London Road, Southampton   *14*
2 17 St George's Drive, Manchester
3 68 Peter Lane, Bristol
4 7 Bush Street, Cambridge
5 21 Oxford Road, Banbury
6 10 Tower Hill, London

⑦ ▣ **Say the phone numbers**

Example: *One*
Two – three – five
nine – eight – double two

1 235 9822   3 991 2341   5 0865 22331
2 334 5377   4 76 22005   6 061 2199

⑧ ▣ **Ask people their phone numbers. Listen and underline any numbers in exercise 7 which are different from what you hear.**

Example: *One*
What's your phone number?
234 9822

*O*ut and About 2

Name? Address? Age? Occupation? - Why so many questions?
What do you know about International food and drink?
Who's who? Women and men at work
Away from home - What do you spend your money on?
Britain in view: Open all hours?
PLUS
What do you do... around the world?

❶ ▦ **Listen to three conversations and number the photos. There is one extra photo.**

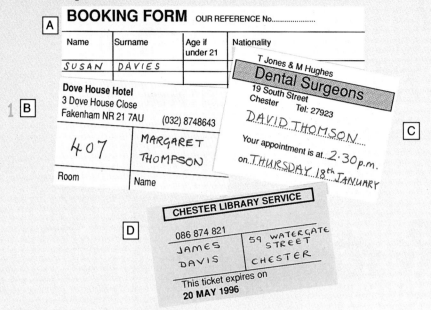

❼ **Look at the photos in WHY SO MANY QUESTIONS? Say which documents you can see.**

passport   driving licence
cheque book   credit card
library ticket   medical card
visitor's ID pass   student's card
membership card

Why
so many
questions?

❷ ▦ **Listen and read.**

RECEPTIONIST   What's your name, please?
MARGARET   My name's Thompson. Margaret Thompson.
RECEPTIONIST   How do you spell that?
MARGARET   T–H–O–M–P–S–O–N.
RECEPTIONIST   Thank you.

❸ ▦ **Listen and repeat.**

<u>spell</u>   <u>how</u> do you <u>spell</u>   <u>How</u> do you <u>spell</u> that?

❹ **Work in pairs. Look at the photos in activity 1. Act out the conversations with Susan Davies and James Davis.**

❺ **Match the questions to the parts of the form.**

a <u>What's</u> your <u>phone</u> number?
b <u>What's</u> your <u>job</u>?
c Are you <u>married</u>?
d <u>What's</u> your <u>surname</u>?

e <u>Where</u> are you <u>from</u>?
f <u>What's</u> your <u>address</u>?
g <u>How</u> <u>old</u> are you?
h <u>What's</u> your <u>first</u> name?

	DOUGLAS BADER SPORTS CENTRE		
1	**First name** Richard	**Age** 35	5
2	**Surname** Scarrow	**Nationality** Canadian	6
3	**Address** 72 St. Margaret's Rd. OXFORD	**Marital Status** Single	7
4	**Telephone number** 492 317	**Occupation** Journalist	8

▦ **Listen and check.**

❻ **Copy the form.**

Now work in pairs. Fill in the form for your partner.

8 How many of these documents have you got? Ask another student.

A Have you got a ... ?
B Yes, I have. / No, I haven't.

Have you got any other documents? What are they?

I've got a ...

hat's your name?
hat's your address?
ow old are you?

ho asks these questions?
nd why?
o they *all* need
is information?

9 What information is in your documents? Complete the chart.

	name	address	age	nationality	family details	job
the State						
the police						
your school/college						
the library						
your doctor						
your place of work						
your bank						
the tax authority						
clubs						
political parties						

Now say who has got what information about you. Why have they got this information? Have they got more information about you?

They've got my address.

10 Write sentences.

1 What's your name?

1 What is your name?
2 My name is ...
3 I am ...
4 What is your address?
5 What is your phone number?
6 I have not got a phone.

11 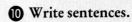 Listen to the questions and spell the words.

Now work in pairs. Choose six words from this lesson. Ask your partner how you spell them.

A How do you spell 'school'?
B S–C–H– double O–L.

In this lesson you practise:
● **Asking for and giving personal details (3)**
● **The present tense:** *be*
● **The present tense:** *have got*
● **Possessive adjectives**
● **Punctuation: Apostrophe**
Now turn to page 32 and look at the STRUCTURES TO LEARN and the WORDS TO REMEMBER.

1 Match the descriptions with the pictures.

A French onion soup

B Russian salad

C an open sandwich

D tortilla

E goulash

F a pizza Napoletana

G fruit salad

1 made with tomatoes and cheese
2 made with eggs and potatoes
3 made with onions and white wine, with bread and cheese
4 made with beef and vegetables
5 made with cold meat, lettuce and tomatoes
6 made with apples, bananas, oranges and grapes
7 made with potatoes, peas and carrots

2 ▣ Listen and repeat.

apples bananas beef bread carrots cheese eggs grapes lettuce meat onions oranges peas potatoes tomatoes vegetables

Write the words that fit these stress patterns.

● •   ● ● •   ● ● •

apples   *bananas*   *oranges*

3 Say what these food items are.

4 ▣ Listen and read.

WAITER Are you ready to order, madam?
WOMAN Yes, I'd like some onion soup and a sandwich, please.
WAITER And for you, sir? What would you like?
MAN What's goulash?
WAITER It's a Hungarian dish, with beef and onions. It's very good.
MAN Yes, all right. I'll have that, please.
WAITER And what would you like to drink?
WOMAN We'd like a bottle of red wine, please.
WAITER Thank you.

5 ▣ Listen and repeat.

like   I'd like
  I'd like some onion soup.
  I'd like a sandwich.
that   I'll have that, please.
drink   What would you like to drink?
wine   red wine
  a bottle of red wine
  We'd like a bottle of red wine.

6 Ask and say what the dishes in activity 1 are.

A What's an open sandwich?
B It's a sandwich with cold meat, lettuce and tomatoes. It's Danish.

❼ Read these phrases.

a bottle of wine

a cup of tea

a pot of tea

a glass of wine

a piece of cake

some chicken

some vegetables

Now make phrases with these words.

beer   coffee   cheese   bread
eggs   meat   milk

❽ Write sentences.

1 *Would you like some French onion soup?*

1 would you like some french onion soup?
2 yes, and i'll have some hungarian goulash.
3 what would you like to drink?
4 we'll have a bottle of italian wine.
5 i'd like a glass of water.

WHAT DO YOU KNOW about International FOOD & DRINK?

A You're in a restaurant. The waiter asks 'Would you like some... ?'

Chow Mein   Coq au Vin   Couscous   Feijoada   Paella   Sukiyaki
Moussaka   Sauerkraut   Toad in the Hole

What do you say?
a Yes, please.   b No, thank you.   c What's...?

B Find out what these dishes are made with. Would you like to change your mind?

C Say what nationality each dish is.
   I think Chow Mein is Chinese.

D You're in a bar. The barman suggests:

☐ a Piña Colada   ☐ Planter's Punch
☐ cheese and onion crisps   ☐ roasted peanuts
☐ a Bloody Mary   ☐ a Molotov cocktail

Do you:
a eat it   b drink it   c call the police?

E Tick the phrases you'd like to learn. Use your dictionary.

I'd like a Coca-Cola and a hamburger, please.
I'd like a typical dish of the region.
I'd like some of that, please.
Is it really dead?
Waiter, **what** is that?
Please telephone a doctor. I don't feel well.

❾ Read WHAT DO YOU KNOW ABOUT INTERNATIONAL FOOD AND DRINK?

❿ Work in groups of three. Write a menu of dishes from this lesson.

STUDENT A   You are a waiter/waitress. Ask Students B and C what they would like to eat and drink.
STUDENTS B AND C   You are in a restaurant. Say what you would like to eat and drink.

⓫ What's your national dish? Find out the English words for its ingredients and write them down.

⓬ Read this lesson again and write down as many words as you can under these headings: *fruit, vegetables, meat, drink.*

In this lesson you practise:
- Asking and saying what dishes are
- Ordering a meal/drink
- Countable and uncountable nouns
- Punctuation: Capital letters

Now turn to page 33 and look at the STRUCTURES TO LEARN and the WORDS TO REMEMBER.

1 🔲 **Listen and read.**

MIKE   Hello, Simon. How are you?
SIMON   Hello, Mike. I'm fine,
    thanks.
MIKE   Alice, this is my friend,
    Simon King. Simon, this is
    Alice Jenkins.
SIMON   How do you do, Miss
    Jenkins? Are you Mike's
    assistant?
ALICE   How do you do, Mr
    King? No, I'm not. I'm an
    accountant.

2 🔲 **Listen and repeat.**

you   How are you?
fine   I'm fine   I'm fine, thanks.
my friend   This is my friend.
do   do you do   How do you do?

3 **Write.**

How are you ?   or   *How do you do ?*

🔲 **Listen and check.**

4 **Say hello to other students and ask how they are.**

5 **Read and find out what an *octopus* is.**

I think it's . . .

6 **Look at the photos in WHO'S WHO? Talk about people's jobs.**

air steward/ess   bank manager
businessman/woman   doctor
engineer   housewife
journalist   musician   nurse
personal assistant   pilot
policeman/woman
postman/woman   secretary
shop assistant   soldier
student   teacher

I think he's a/an . . .
I think she's a/an . . .
I think they're . . .
I don't know.

7 **Work in pairs.**

STUDENT A   Turn to page 110
for your instructions.
STUDENT B   Turn to page 112
for your instructions.

8 **Work in pairs. Ask and say what people's jobs are.**

A What does Kenneth Hill do?
B He's a . . .

B What's Holly West's job?
A She's a . . .

9 **Think about doctors, nurses, engineers, bank managers, personal assistants, pilots in your country. Are they men, women, or both?**

10 **Match personal pronouns with possessive adjectives.**

Personal pronouns: subject	Possessive adjectives
I	your
you	their
he	our
she	its
it	my
we	his
they	her

Who's Who?

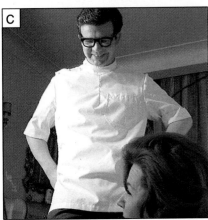

⓫ **Ask for and give more information about the people in the photos.**

What's Greg Murphy's/Mary Tyler's address?
What's his/her/their telephone number?
How do you spell his/her surname?

⓬ **Work in groups. One person thinks of a job and mimes it. Now ask and say what the job is.**

A Are you a/an . . . ?
B Yes, I am./No, I'm not.

A Is he/she a/an . . . ?
B Yes, he is./No, she isn't.

⓭ **Write sentences.**

1 *What's Joan's job ?*
 What's her job ?

1 Joan/job
2 Holly/address
3 Mary/phone number
4 Henry/address
5 Kenneth/job
6 Rodney and Anna/address

⓮ **Find three English words which you don't understand. Ask another student or your teacher what they mean.**

A I don't understand 'journalist'. What does it mean?
B It's someone who writes for a newspaper.

A What does 'octopus' mean?
B It's got eight legs, like this.

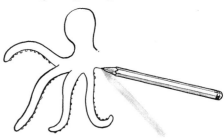

In this lesson you practise:
● **Meeting people**
● **Greeting people**
● **Expressing opinions (1)**
● **Asking for and giving personal details (4)**
● **Personal pronouns: Subject**
● **Possessive adjectives**
● **Possessive form of nouns**
● **The present tense:** *be*
Now turn to page 34 and look at the STRUCTURES TO LEARN and the WORDS TO REMEMBER.

❶ Look at the photo. Which of these items can you see?

apples newspaper orange juice bread cheese biscuits sugar toothpaste train tickets stamps tomatoes coffee postcards cigarettes wine bag shoes butter guide book suncream grapes dress T-shirt map magazine soap hotel bill restaurant bill water ice-cream

❷ ▣ Listen and read.

A There isn't any sugar.
B That's right.

B There's some water.
A Yes, there is.

A There aren't any postcards.
B Yes, there are!

B There are some grapes.
A No, there aren't!

A There's a bag.
B Yes, OK.

B There isn't a magazine.
A Good.

▣ **Now listen again and repeat.**

❸ Work in pairs.

STUDENT A Turn to page 110 for your instructions.
STUDENT B Turn to page 112 for your instructions.

❹ Divide the items in activity 1 into countable and uncountable items.

countable uncountable
apples orange juice

❺ Complete the sentences with *a*, *some* or *any*. Finish with a full stop (.) or a question mark (?).

1 Have you got . . . cheese
2 There isn't . . . soap
3 Could I have . . . bottle of milk
4 I haven't got . . . oranges
5 I'd like . . . toothpaste

❻ ▣ Listen and read.

CUSTOMER Could I have a map, please? How much is it?
SHOP ASSISTANT Ninety-nine pence.
CUSTOMER And I'd like some postcards. How much are they?
ASSISTANT Twenty pence each.
CUSTOMER Have you got any suncream?
ASSISTANT Yes, it's over there.

Now listen again and repeat

❼ Match the prices with the items in the photo.

thirty pence   fifty-five pence
ninety-nine pence   twenty pence each
thirty-four pence each   one pound fifty-five
seventy pence   two pounds forty-nine

Now work in pairs. Ask and say the prices.

How much is the bread?
How much are the cigarettes?

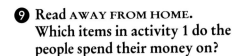
8 Look at the photos in AWAY FROM HOME. What do you think the people spend their money on when they're on holiday?

What do you spend your money on away from home?

Marta de Groot
I spend my money on food and travel. I don't eat in restaurants. I haven't got much money and restaurants are too expensive. I buy water, fruit and food for sandwiches. And I go everywhere by coach or by train. The only other things I buy are a map and some postcards. But no stamps! I take the postcards home with me.

Heinrich and Hildegarde Feldmann
We go to restaurants and bars, and I like a newspaper as well. We don't buy books, we bring them from home. We usually buy postcards and presents for our children, perhaps some T-shirts or other souvenirs. My husband needs his cigarettes too. We pay for the hotel by credit card. Oh, and we take home some local food and a bottle of something to drink.

Mirella Bianco
I always buy something typical, like a leather bag or shoes. I love clothes, so I go to places where the shops are good. I buy a good guide book but no newspapers. I don't want to read the news when I'm on holiday. I usually get something for the beach, like suncream. And I love ice-cream!

9 Read AWAY FROM HOME. Which items in activity 1 do the people spend their money on?

10 Write a paragraph about what you spend your money on when you're on holiday. Use the paragraphs in AWAY FROM HOME to help you.

11 What do you do when you don't know a word?

Work in pairs.
STUDENT A   You're in a shop. Think of something you want to buy and mime it to Student B.
STUDENT B   You're a shop assistant. Student A wants to buy something. What is it?

I'd like a . . .
Have you got any . . . ?
Could I have a . . . ?

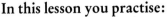

In this lesson you practise:
- **Asking and saying how much things cost (1)**
- **Asking for things**
- **Saying what there is**
- *some* and *any*
- **Articles:** *the*
- **Punctuation: full stops and question marks**

Now turn to page 35 and look at the STRUCTURES TO LEARN and the WORDS TO REMEMBER.

❶ Match the times with the clocks.

A B C D

a quarter to four   nine o'clock
eleven o'clock   half past five
a quarter past ten   half past six
a quarter past two   two o'clock

Now draw the missing clocks.

❷ ▭ Listen and repeat.

what's	the	time?
nine	o'	clock
half	past	five
a quarter	to	four
a quarter	past	ten

Now write and say.

2.30   7.45   7.15   4.00

2.30 –
half past two

❸ Look at the clocks in activity 1. Ask and say the time.

A What's the time?
B It's half past five.

❹ Read LIFESTYLE PROFILE and complete the chart for Renate and Kevin.

❺ Work in pairs.

STUDENT A   Turn to page 110 for your instructions.
STUDENT B   Turn to page 112 for your instructions.

❻ Ask and answer questions about Dean and Rosa.

A What time does Dean get up?
B *At* half past ten./*At* ten thirty.

A What time does he have breakfast/lunch/dinner?
B *At* . . .

❼ Complete the paragraph about Renate.

Renate gets up at . . . and she has breakfast at . . . . She starts . . . at . . . and has . . . at one o'clock. She finishes work at . . . . She . . . dinner at . . . and she goes to . . . at . . . .

Lifestyle profile *What time do you get up? When do you go to bed? What time do you start work? When do you finish? Different people have different lifestyles . . .*

Renate
Renate is a travel agent in Munich. 'I have breakfast at a quarter past seven. I start work at eight o'clock in the morning, and I finish at half past five in the evening. I have lunch at one o'clock, and dinner at half past seven. I go to bed at midnight, and I get up at a quarter past six. I like my job, but I don't like getting up early.'

Kevin
Kevin is a taxi-driver in Dublin. 'I start work at a quarter to eleven at night, and finish at half past six in the morning. I like working at night. I have breakfast at seven o'clock. Then I go to bed at about a quarter to eight and get up at two o'clock in the afternoon. I don't have lunch but I have dinner with the family at six o'clock.'

	Renate	Kevin	Rosa	Dean	you	your partner
get up	6.15					
have breakfast						
go to work/ school						
have lunch						
leave work/ school						
have dinner						
go to bed						

❽ Write the *he/she* form of these verbs.

go   get up   have   start   finish

❾ Complete the chart for *you*.

Now work in pairs. Complete the chart for *your partner*.

A What time do you . . .?
B . . . *in* the morning/*in* the afternoon/*in* the evening/*at* night

Now write a paragraph about your partner.

10 Look at BRITAIN IN VIEW.
Match the photos with the places.

post office   bank   pub
shop   supermarket

11 Find out which places are open at these times.

6.00 on Friday evening
8.30 on Monday morning
3.15 on Wednesday afternoon
7.30 on Sunday evening
12.00 on Saturday night

6 pm: pubs, supermarkets

12 Say what times places open and close in your country.

In my country, banks open at eight o'clock in the morning.

13 Ask and say the times.

A How do you say this in English?

B Nine five *or* Five past nine.

A What's this in English?

B Two fifty *or* Ten to three.

A How do you say this?

B Six thirty-five *or* Twenty-five to seven.

Now ask about these times.

5.20   8.55   4.40   3.10   7.25

In this lesson you practise:
● **Asking and saying the time**
● **Asking and saying what time people do things**
● **The present simple tense**
● **Prepositions of time:** *in, at*
Now turn to page 36 and look at the STRUCTURES TO LEARN and the WORDS TO REMEMBER.

Britain in view

open all hours?

It's six o'clock on Friday evening. Is Britain still open?

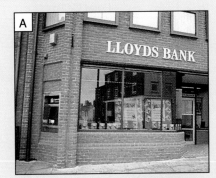

	open	close	days
post offices	9.00am 9.00am	5.30pm 12.30pm	Mon–Fri Sat
banks	9.30am 9.30am	3.30pm 12.30pm	Mon–Fri Sat
pubs	11.00am 12.00am 7.00pm	11.00pm 3.00pm 10.30pm	Mon–Sat Sun
shops	9.00am	5.30pm	Mon–Sat
supermarkets	8.00am	8.00pm	Mon–Sat

❶ Talk to four people in your class. Ask questions about their:

– name
– address
– telephone number
– nationality
– marital status
– family
– job

❷ Look at WHAT DO YOU DO ... AROUND THE WORLD? Ask and say what nationality the people are. Choose from these nationalities.

Brazilian   British   Chilean
Chinese   Canadian   Danish
French   German   Malaysian
Spanish   Thai   Uruguayan

❸ Ask and say what the people in the photos do.

A   What's Peter's job?
B   I think he's a policeman.

A   What does Anne do?
B   I think she's an air stewardess.

A   What's Lin-Lin's job?
B   I don't know.

▭▭ **Listen and check.**

❹ Match the questions.

1 What's your job?
2 What's her address?
3 What's her job?
4 What's their job?
5 What's their address?
6 What's his address?

a Where does he live?
b What do you do?
c What does she do?
d Where does she live?
e What do they do?
f Where do they live?

What do you do... around the world?

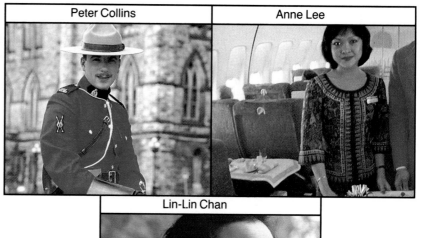

Peter Collins   Anne Lee

Lin-Lin Chan

Lars Andersen   Jacques Mavel

❺ Work in pairs.

STUDENT A   Make a list of six things you need to buy. Visit Student B's shop and do your shopping. As you buy things, tick your list.
STUDENT B   You work in a shop. Make a list of twelve things you sell. Sell things to Student A.

A Could I have some/a ...?/I'd like some/a ...
B I'm sorry, I haven't got any ...

A Have you got any ...?
B Yes, I have./No, I'm sorry, I haven't. I've got some ...

6 Write the times you do these activities.

have dinner   get up
finish work/school   go to bed
have breakfast
start school/work   have lunch

Now find people who do the activities at the same time.

A Do you get up at seven?
B Yes, I do. / No, I don't. I get up at eight o'clock.

7 ▭ Listen to Ellen talking about a day in the life of New York. Circle the times you hear.

3am   5am   7am   8am   8.30am
8.45am   9am   10am   11am   12am   1pm   2pm   3pm   4pm
4.30pm   5pm   6pm   6.30pm   7pm   8pm   9pm   10pm   11pm

8 Say what happens in Ellen's day. Talk about yourself.

Ellen usually starts work at half past eight, but I usually start work at nine o'clock.

9 Look at these parts of a letter from a penfriend. Put the parts in order.

a   My mother and father live in London. I've got a brother and a sister. My brother is an accountant and my sister is a student. I'm not married.
I get up at seven o'clock and have breakfast.

b   Tell me about yourself. How old are you? What do you do? Where do you live? Tell me about your family. Tell me about a day in your life. Please write soon.
Best wishes.
Pat

c   Then I go to work in Windsor at a quarter past eight and start work at nine o'clock. I have lunch at one o'clock, and go home at about five o'clock. I have dinner at seven and then I see friends or stay at home and watch TV. I go to bed at about eleven o'clock.

d   34, Mill Road,
Maidenhead,
BERKSHIRE,
England.
28 February 1990

Dear...,
My name's Pat Jones, and I'm a personal assistant to a bank manager. I'm from Wales, but I live in Berkshire, England. I'm twenty-two.

10 Write a reply to Pat's letter.

11 ▭ Listen to three situations. Answer the questions.

1 How many people do you hear in each situation?
2 Are they men or women?
3 How old are they?
4 Where are they?

12 Read these letters.

ANY QUESTIONS?

WRITE TO THE LANGUAGE DOCTOR

QUESTION   When do you say good morning, good afternoon, good evening, good night and goodbye?
Pierre, Marseilles

ANSWER   You say good morning until 12 noon, good afternoon until about 5pm and good evening after that.
  You say goodbye when you leave someone. You usually say good morning, good afternoon and good evening when you arrive, but you can sometimes use these expressions when you leave (in shops and restaurants, for example). You only say good night when you leave.

Have you got any questions about English? Write a letter to the language doctor and give it to your teacher.

STRUCTURES TO LEARN

Asking for and giving personal details (3)

Present tense: *be*

Full form	Short form
My name *is* Susan.	My name's Susan.
I *am* nineteen.	I'*m* nineteen.
What *is* your name?	What's your name?
How old *are* you?	–
Where *are* you from?	–
Are you married?	–

See also *Lesson 8 LANGUAGE STUDY*.

Present tense: *have got*

Affirmative

Full form	Short form
I have got a driving licence.	I've got a driving licence.
They have got my address.	They've got my address.

Questions	Short answers
Have you got a credit card?	Yes, I have. No, I haven't.

See also *Lesson 12 LANGUAGE STUDY*.

Punctuation: Apostrophe

You use the short form of verbs when speaking and often when writing English. You put an apostrophe (') to show that a letter or letters are missing.

Full form	Short form
What is your name?	What's your name?
My name is Simon.	My name's Simon.
What is your phone number?	What's your phone number?
I have not got a phone.	I haven't got a phone.

Possessive adjectives

My name's John. (I'm John.)
Your name's Pat. (You're Pat.)

See also *Lesson 8 LANGUAGE STUDY*.

WORDS TO REMEMBER

first name /fɜ:st neɪm/   single /sɪŋgəl/
surname /sɜ:neɪm/

cheque book /tʃɛkbʊk/   credit card /krɛdɪt kɑ:d/
driving licence /draɪvɪŋ laɪsəns/
library ticket /laɪbri tɪkɪt/
medical card /mɛdɪkəl kɑ:d/
membership card /mɛmbəʃɪp kɑ:d/
passport /pɑ:spɔ:t/   student's card /stju:dənts kɑ:d/

bank /bæŋk/   club /clʌb/   library /laɪbri/
police /pəli:s/   school /sku:l/   state /steɪt/

PRACTICE EXERCISES

❶ 📼 **Listen and number the words you hear.**

Example: *One: P–O–L–I–C–E*

address   bank   card   club   doctor   form
library   name   number   passport   police 1 school

❷ **Write questions. Underline the most important words.**

Example: 1   *What's your name* ?

1 name   3 phone number   5 job
2 address   4 nationality   6 married

📼 **Now listen and check. Repeat the questions. The stressed words are the most important words.**

❸ 📼 **Listen to the conversation and tick the correct answers.**

Tom Hodge	Tim Hedge ✓
14 Library Lane	40 Library Road
721314	721315
Australia	Canada
engineer	teacher
yes	no

❹ **Write** *I, my, you,* **or** *your.*

JOHN   Hello, what's . . . name?
STEPHEN   . . . 'm Stephen Anthony. Stephen is . . . first name and Anthony is . . . surname.
JOHN   How old are . . . ?
STEPHEN   . . . 'm twenty-five.
JOHN   What do . . . do?
STEPHEN   . . . 'm a student.
JOHN   Are . . . married?
STEPHEN   Yes, . . . am.

📼 **Listen and check.**

STRUCTURES TO LEARN

Asking and saying what dishes are
What's tortilla?
It's made with eggs and potatoes.

Ordering a meal/drink

What would you like to eat/drink?	I'd like some fruit salad. I'll have a cup of coffee.

Countable nouns
Countable nouns have a singular and a plural form.
You use *a/an* for singular countable nouns and *some* for plural countable nouns.

Singular	Plural
a carrot	some carrots
an apple	some apples

Uncountable nouns
Uncountable nouns do not usually have a singular or plural form. You use *some* with uncountable nouns.
some tea
some wine
some cake

Punctuation: Capital letters
You use a capital letter in these situations:
The first letter of the first word in a sentence.
The first person singular *I*.
Names of people, countries, towns and nationalities: *Mrs Archer, France, London, Hungarian goulash*

WORDS TO REMEMBER

eat /iːt/   drink /drɪŋk/

apple /ˈæpəl/   banana /bəˈnɑːnə/   beef /biːf/
bread /brɛd/   cake /keɪk/   carrot /ˈkærət/
cheese /tʃiːz/   chicken /ˈtʃɪkɪn/   egg /ɛg/
food /fuːd/   fruit /fruːt/   grape /greɪp/
lettuce /ˈlɛtɪs/   meat /miːt/   onion /ˈʌnjən/
orange/ ˈɒrɪndʒ/   pea /piː/   pizza /ˈpiːtsə/
potato /pəˈteɪtəʊ/   salad /ˈsæləd/
sandwich /ˈsænwɪtʃ/   soup /suːp/
tomato /təˈmɑːtəʊ/   vegetable /ˈvɛdʒtəbəl/

beer /bɪə/   coca cola /ˈkəʊkəˌkəʊlə/   coffee /ˈkɒfi/
milk /mɪlk/   tea /tiː/   water /ˈwɔːtə/
wine /waɪn/

bottle /ˈbɒtəl/   cup /kʌp/   glass /glɑːs/
piece /piːs/   pot /pɒt/

PRACTICE EXERCISES

1 Which words have two syllables? Which words have three syllables?

apples 2   bananas 3   carrots
lettuce   onions   oranges
potatoes   tomatoes   vegetables

▭▭ Now listen and check. Repeat the words.

2 ▭▭ Listen and repeat. Make sure your voice rises ↗ and falls ↘ with the arrows.

1 What would you like to eat?

2 I'd like some onion soup.

3 I'll have a sandwich.

4 What would you like to drink?

5 I'd like a cup of tea.

Now read the sentences aloud.

3 Match the dishes with the countries.

1 Moussaka   Algeria
2 Chow Mein   Spain
3 Couscous   Greece
4 Paella   China
5 Sauerkraut   Germany

▭▭ Answer questions about the dishes.

Example: *What's Moussaka?*
         It's a Greek dish.

4 Write *a, an* or *some*.

peas   open sandwich   cup of tea   water
potatoes   beef   piece of cheese   onion

▭▭ Listen and check. Repeat the phrases.

5 Complete the dialogue.

WAITER   Are you ready . . . order, sir?
MAN   Yes, I'd like . . . sandwich and . . . glass of beer, please.
WAITER   And what would you . . . , madam?
WOMAN   I'll . . . some tomato soup, please.
WAITER   And what . . . you have . . . drink?
WOMAN   A glass . . . water, please.

Underline the most important words.

▭▭ Now listen and check. The stressed words are the most important words.

STRUCTURES TO LEARN

Meeting people
This is Simon King.
How do you do?

Greeting people
How are you?
I'm fine, thanks.

Expressing opinions (1)
I think he's a doctor.   I don't know.

See also *Lessons 24, 28 and 29 LANGUAGE STUDY*.

Asking for and giving personal details (4)

What does Anna do?	She's a doctor.
What's Greg's / his job?	He's an engineer.
What's Holly's / her job?	She's a policewoman.
What's Greg and Mary's their phone number?	It's 987654.

Personal pronouns: Subject
I   you   he   she   it   we   they

Possessive adjectives
my   your   his   her   its   our   their

Possessive form of nouns
You can add apostrophe s (-'s) to singular nouns and nouns with an irregular plural to show possession.
Greg's address   (the address of Greg)
the children's mother   (the mother of the children)

You add an apostrophe ' to plural nouns.
the students' teacher   (the teacher of the students)

Present tense: *be*

Affirmative

Full form	Short form
I am	I'm
you are	you're
he is	he's
she is	she's
it is	it's
we are	we're
they are	they're

Negative

Full form	Short form
I am not	I'm not
you are not	you aren't
he is not	he isn't
she is not	she isn't
it is not	it isn't
we are not	we aren't
they are not	they aren't

Questions / **Short answers**

Questions	Short answers	
Am I...?	Yes, I am.	No, I'm not.
Are you...?	Yes, you are.	No, you aren't.
Is he...?	Yes, he is.	No, he isn't.
Is she...?	Yes, she is.	No, she isn't.
Is it...?	Yes, it is.	No, it isn't.
Are we...?	Yes, we are.	No, we aren't.
Are they...?	Yes, they are.	No, they aren't.

WORDS TO REMEMBER

air steward /ɛə stjʊəd/   air stewardess /ɛə stjʊədɛs/
bank manager /bæŋk mænɪdʒə/
businessman /bɪznɪsmən/
businesswoman /bɪznɪswʊmən/
housewife /haʊswaɪf/   journalist /dʒɜːnəlɪst/
musician /mjuːzɪʃən/   nurse /nɜːs/
personal assistant /pɜːsənəl əsɪstənt/
pilot /paɪlət/   policeman /pəliːsmən/
policewoman /pəliːswʊmən/   postman /pəʊstmən/
postwoman /pəʊstwʊmən/   soldier /səʊldʒə/

Mr /mɪstə/   Mrs /mɪsɪz/   Miss /mɪs/   Ms /mɪz/

mean /miːn/   understand /ʌndəstænd/

PRACTICE EXERCISES

❶ **Count the syllables in each word.**

accountant 3   assistant   doctor   journalist
musician   pilot   policeman   soldier   student

▰▰▰ **Which words have the stress pattern ●●●?**
Listen and check. Repeat the words.

❷ **Write** I, *my, you, your, he, his, she, her, we, our,* *they*, **or** *their*.

1 I know Mary is married. But what's ... surname?
2 Where do ... live, Jane? I mean, what's ... address
3 I've got Greg's address, but I haven't got...
   telephone number.
4 ... live with ... husband in Toronto. ...
   telephone number is 887911.
5 Doug, this is ... friend, Kate. ... husband is
   James Black, the journalist. ... live in New York.

▰▰▰ **Listen and check.**

❸ ▰▰▰ **Ask questions. Listen to the answers and**
match the people with the occupations.

Example: *Jill*
          What does Jill do?
          She's a journalist.

1 Jill	doctor
2 Andrea	journalist
3 Kyoko	policeman
4 Claudia and Luigi	students
5 Tom	musician

❹ ▰▰▰ **Answer the questions about the people in**
exercise 3.

Example: What's *Jill's job?*
          She's a journalist.

STRUCTURES TO LEARN

Asking and saying how much things cost (1)

How much is the bread? Fifty-five pence.
How much are the cigarettes? One pound fifty-five.

Asking for things
Could I have a ticket?
I'd like some toothpaste.
Have you got any postcards?

Saying what there is
There's a bag.
There are some stamps.
There isn't any sugar.
There aren't any apples.

Affirmative		Negative	
Full form	**Short form**	**Full form**	**Short form**
There is	There's	There is not	There isn't
There are	–	There are not	There aren't

Questions	Short answers	
Is there . . . ?	Yes, there is.	No, there isn't.
Are there . . . ?	Yes, there are.	No, there aren't.

some and any
You use *some* in affirmative sentences.
There's *some* water.
There are *some* apples.

You use *any* in negative sentences.
There isn't *any* sugar.
There aren't *any* postcards.

You usually use *any* in questions.
Is there *any* water?
Are there *any* apples?

But you say:
Could I have *some* milk, please?
Could I have *some* stamps, please?

Articles: the
The definite article is *the*. You say /ðə/ before a consonant.
the bag   *the* guide book

You say /ði:/ before a vowel.
the apple   *the* ice-cream

Punctuation: Full stops and question marks
You put a full stop at the end of every statement.
You put a question mark at the end of every question.
Could I have a map, please?
How much is it?

WORDS TO REMEMBER

bag /bæg/   bar /bɑ:/   bill /bɪl/   biscuit /bɪskɪt/
cigarette /sɪgərɛt/   dress /drɛs/
guide book /gaɪd bʊk/   hotel /həʊtɛl/
ice-cream /aɪs kri:m/   magazine /mægəzi:n/
map /mæp/   money /mʌni/   newspaper /nju:zpeɪpə/
orange juice /ɒrɪndʒ dʒu:s/   postcard /pəʊskɑ:d/
restaurant /rɛstərɒn/   shoe /ʃu:/   soap /səʊp/
souvenir /su:vənɪə/   stamp /stæmp/
sun cream /sʌn kri:m/   toothpaste /tu:θpeɪst/
train ticket /treɪn tɪkət/   T-shirt /ti: ʃɜ:t/

That's right /ðæts raɪt/   OK /əʊkeɪ/

PRACTICE EXERCISES

❶ Underline the stressed syllables.

newspaper   biscuits   toothpaste   coffee
souvenir   sugar   water   butter   money

▭▭ **Listen and check. Repeat the words.**

❷ Write *a*, *an*, *some* or *any*.

1 I haven't got . . . stamps.
2 I'd like . . . cheese, please.
3 Have you got . . . map?
4 Could I have . . . grapes?
5 There isn't . . . water.

▭▭ **Listen and check.**

❸ ▭▭ Ask questions. Listen and match the items with the prices.

Example: *cheese*
How much is the cheese?
One pound eighty.

1 cheese	4 grapes	£29.99	45p
2 shoes	5 newspaper	90p	£3.25
3 wine	6 biscuits	£1.80 1	35p

❹ ▭▭ Answer questions about the items in exercise 3.

Example: *How much is the cheese?*
One pound eighty.

❺ ▭▭ Ask questions. Listen to the answers and tick or cross the items.

Example: *bread*
Have you got any bread?
No, I'm sorry.

1 bread ✗   2 cigarettes   3 toothpaste
4 tomatoes   5 postcards   6 orange juice

STRUCTURES TO LEARN

Asking and saying the time
What's the time?   It's ten o'clock.

Asking and saying what time people do things
You use the present simple tense to ask and say what time people do things.

Present simple tense

Affirmative	Negative	
	Full form	**Short form**
I start	I do not start	I don't start
you start	you do not start	you don't start
he/she/it starts	he/she/it does not start	he/she/it doesn't start
we start	we do not start	we don't start
they start	they do not start	they don't start

Questions

Do I/you/we/they start . . .?
Does he/she/it start . . .?

Third person singular (he/she/it) affirmative
You form the third person singular (*he, she, it*) of most verbs in affirmative sentences with -*s*.
    I get up at half past seven.
    He/She gets up at half past seven.
    I start work at nine o'clock.
    He/She starts work at nine o'clock.

You add -*es* to *do*, *go*, and verbs which end in -*ch*, -*ss*, -*sh*, or -*x*.
    He goes to work at half past eight.
    She finishes school at half past three.

have is an irregular verb. The third person singular is *has*.
    She *has* lunch at half past one.

Questions
You form questions in the present simple tense with *do/does*.
    What time *do* you
    When *does* he/she   get up?
    What time *do* post offices open/close?

Prepositions of time: *in, at*
    in the morning   *at* five o'clock
    in the afternoon   *at* half past seven
    in the evening   *at* night

For more prepositions of time, see *Lessons 13, 17 and 19 LANGUAGE STUDY*.

WORDS TO REMEMBER

o'clock /əklɒk/   a quarter past /ə kwɔːtə pɑːs/
half past /hɑːf pɑːs/   a quarter to /ə kwɔːtə tə/
a.m. /ɛɪɛm/   p.m. /piːɛm/   morning /mɔːnɪŋ/
afternoon /ɑːftənuːn/   evening /iːvnɪŋ/
night /naɪt/

have breakfast /hæv brɛkfəst/
have lunch /hæv lʌntʃ/   have dinner /hæv dɪnə/
get up /gɛt ʌp/   start work /stɑːt wɜːk/
finish school /fɪnɪʃ skuːl/
go to bed /gəʊ tə bɛd/   open /əʊpən/
close /kləʊz/

post office /pəʊst ɒfɪs/   pub /pʌb/   shop /ʃɒp/
supermarket /suːpəmɑːkɪt/

PRACTICE EXERCISES

❶ **Look at the stressed words in these phrases.**

twenty-five to one   five past two

Underline the stressed words in these phrases.

half past four   a quarter to seven   five to five
twenty past eight   ten to six   twenty-five to nine

▭ **Listen and check. Repeat the phrases.**

❷ **Say the time in another way.**

Example: *Seven thirty.*
            Half past seven.

7.30   2.45   4.20   11.25   5.55   9.10

❸ **Complete the sentences.**

    1 Steve . . . up at seven o'clock. (get)
    2 Most people . . . to work at nine. (go)
    3 Jill . . . work at ten o'clock. (start)
    4 My parents . . . dinner at six o'clock. (have)
    5 When do post offices . . .? (open)

▭ **Listen and check.**

❹ ▭ **Ask questions. Listen and write the times.**

Example: *banks/open*
            What time do banks open?
            At nine thirty.

    1 banks/open 9.30   4 pubs/close
    2 post offices/close   5 supermarkets/open
    3 people/start work   6 shops/close

Now write sentences.

Example: 1 *Banks open at 9.30.*

*L*ifestyle 3

What do you like doing in your free time?
Britain in view: From caravan to castle
On the town - entertainment for all tastes
On holiday in... San Francisco
What do your clothes say about you?
PLUS
Find out why so many people speak English

1 📼 **Listen and number the kinds of music you hear.**

blues   classical music   country and western music   disco music
folk music   jazz   opera   reggae   rock music   samba

2 📼 **Listen and read.**

NICOLA   Do you like this music?
ROGER   Not very much. I don't like jazz.
NICOLA   What kind of music do you like?
ROGER   I like classical music.
NICOLA   And do you like going to concerts?
ROGER   Yes, I do. I love it.
NICOLA   So do I.

3 📼 **Listen and repeat.**

music   Do you like this music?
Not very much.   jazz   I don't like jazz.
what kind of music   What kind of music do you like?
I like classical music.
concerts   going to concerts   Do you like going to concerts?
Yes, I do.   I love it.
So do I.

4 **Ask four students what kind of music they like.**

A Do you like jazz?
B Yes, I do./Not very much./No, I don't.

A What kind of music do you like?
B I like rock music *and* folk music./I don't like opera *or* classical music.

5 **Ask and say what kind of music people in your class like.**

A What kind of music does Anna like?
B She likes reggae *and* samba, *but* she doesn't like rock music *or* blues.

Find out what kind of music most people like.

6 **Look at the pictures. What activities can you see? Choose from these words and phrases.**

playing football/tennis
running   swimming   reading
cooking   watching TV
writing letters   listening to music
going out with friends
going to parties/discos   dancing
going to the theatre/cinema
going to concerts/restaurants

📼 **Now listen to five sounds. Which activities can you hear? Number the activities in the order you hear them.**

what do you like doing in your
FREE TIME?

Do you like running? Do you like writing letters? Do you like dancing? Three people talk about what they like doing in their free time.

Mary

Tom

Shelley

Pat

1 'Well, I like watching and playing football. Most of all, I like meeting friends after the match. It's the social element I like. And I like swimming and all sorts of sports. I don't like just sitting at home doing nothing.'

2 'Me? Well, I like being with lots of people. I don't like being on my own. I like going out with friends, going to parties, discos, that sort of thing. I always try and make sure I've got plenty of things to do at the weekend.'

3 'We can't go out too much because of the children. We don't like leaving them. But I love playing with them, taking them to the park at weekends. And I like cooking and writing letters . . . but with three young children I don't have much time!'

---

7 Read the paragraphs in WHAT DO YOU LIKE DOING IN YOUR FREE TIME? and match them with the photos. There is one extra photo.

8 Now ask and say what the people like doing.

  A What does (name) like doing?
  B He/She likes . . .

9 Ask other students what they like doing. Say what you like doing.

  A What do you like doing in your free time?
  B I like . . .
  A So do I./Do you? I don't.

  A Do you like . . .?
  B No, I don't.
  A Nor do I./Don't you? I do.

10 Write the '-ing' form of these verbs.

  cook go listen play read
  dance have leave write
  run sit swim

  Look at the spelling.

11 Work in groups of four. Find three things you all like doing, and three things you don't like doing.

  A Do you like . . .?
  B Yes, I do./Yes, I love it./ No, I don't./Not very much./It's all right.

  Now write a paragraph about your likes and dislikes.

  We all like reading but we don't like watching TV.

12 Write questions.

  1 Do you like jazz ?

  1 you/like/jazz
  2 he/like/disco music
  3 they/like/samba
  4 she/like/go to concerts
  5 what/you/like/do
  6 what/they/like/do

13 Find an English song which you like. Play the record or cassette, or sing it to the class. Do other students like it too?

> In this lesson you practise:
> • Asking and saying what people like and like doing
> Now turn to page 50 and look at the STRUCTURES TO LEARN and the WORDS TO REMEMBER.

Britain in view

from caravan to castle

An Englishman's home is his castle -or is it? In Britain some people live in castles, and others...

The King's bedroom at Belvoir Castle

A kitchen in Glasgow

The garden at Blenheim Palace

A bathroom in Cardiff

The dining room at Blickling Park

A sitting room in Kent

❶ Read these words and find five rooms. Look at BRITAIN IN VIEW to help you.

armchair basin bath bathroom bed bedroom chair cooker
cupboard dining room door fridge garden kitchen shower
sink sitting room sofa stairs table television toilet
wardrobe window

▄▄ **Now listen and check. Repeat the words.**

❷ ▄▄ Listen to three conversations. Complete the chart for Steve and for Lucy and Jack.

	Helen	Steve	Lucy and Jack
house	✓		
flat			
bedrooms	3		
bathroom	✓		
kitchen	✓		
sitting room	✓		
dining room	✓		
toilet			
garden	✗		

❸ ▄▄ Listen and read.

A Does Helen live in a house?
B Yes, she does.
A Has it got a dining room?
B Yes, it has.
A Is there a garden?
B No, there isn't.
A How many bedrooms are there?
B Three.

Now listen again and repeat.

❹ Ask and answer questions about the people in activity 2.

A Does he live in a flat?
B Yes, he does.

A Do they live in a flat?
B No, they don't.

A Is there a dining room?
B Yes, there is.

A Has it got a garden?
B No, it hasn't.

A How many bedrooms has it got?
B One.

5 **Talk about your homes.**

A Do you live in a house or a flat?

B I live in a house.

6 **Write a question for each answer.**

1 Yes, it has.   3 Yes, there is.
2 No, it hasn't.   4 No, there isn't.

7 **Look at the words in activity 1. Find the equipment and furniture words. Then match the words with the pictures.**

8 **Work in pairs. Say the rooms where you can find the furniture.**

A   cooker
B   kitchen

9 **Work in pairs. Look at the BRITAIN IN VIEW photos.**

STUDENT A   Choose a photo but don't point at it. Say what you can see.
STUDENT B   Listen and point at the right photo.

10 **Work in pairs. Talk about the rooms and furniture in your homes.**

Now write a paragraph about your partner's home.

Carlo lives in a small house in Perugia. Downstairs, it's got a kitchen and a sitting room, but it hasn't got a dining room. There's a cooker, a fridge and a sink in the kitchen, and there are four chairs and a table

11 **Read this address.**

Mr Oliver Kenny,
2, Treetop Road,
Haslemere,
Surrey HA5 9PN

Now write these addresses.

1 ms helen marsh 7 oaks street manchester m13 7kn
2 mr and mrs j lambert 34 lennard road bristol bs6 8yh
3 miss f newman 222 king street london sw9 7gh
4 mr g harris the manor house park road edinburgh scotland
5 s donovan flat 1 89 oxford road reading oxfordshire rg3 6jk

12 **Match the words with the phonetic spellings.**

kitchen   sofa   cooker   cupboard   table
/kʌbəd/   /teɪbəl/   /kɪtʃɪn/   kʊkə/   səʊfə/

Now point at the words. Ask and say how you pronounce them.

How do you pronounce this word?

Ask other students about five words in Lessons 11 and 12.

How do you pronounce T–E–L–E–V–I–S–I–O–N?

Say these words.

/mjuːzɪk/   /kwɔːtə/   /lʌntʃ/   /fəʊn/   /hʌzbənd/

> In this lesson you practise:
> ● **Talking about people's homes**
> ● **The present tense:** *have got*
> Now turn to page 51 and look at the STRUCTURES TO LEARN and the WORDS TO REMEMBER.

❶ **Match the words with the photos in** LIFESTYLE ON THE TOWN.

exhibition   play   film   concert

❷ **Read** LIFESTYLE ON THE TOWN.

Now ask and say.

STUDENT A
How often do you go to . . .?
– the cinema
– the theatre
– concerts.
– art exhibitions

STUDENT B
I go to the cinema twice a week.
I never go to the theatre.
I go to concerts about
  once a month.
I go to art exhibitions about
  three times a year.

A

B

LIFESTYLE

ON THE TOWN

How often do you go to the cinema? How often do you go to the theatre? Do you ever go to concerts or art exhibitions? There's so much to do, you say, and so little time! But there's always time to enjoy yoursel

❸ **Match the words in activity 1 with the four events below.**

– International Festival of Street Music
– *A Midsummer Night's Dream* by William Shakespeare
– Late Picasso
– *Cry Freedom* (Richard Attenborough, 1987)

Now match the four events with the places in the chart. Complete the
What's on? **column.**

What's on?	Where?	When?	How much?
	Open Air Theatre	Mon, Tue, Wed 7.45pm Wed mat 2.30pm	
	Riverside Studios Cinema		£2.80
International Festival of Street Music	Queen Elizabeth Hall		Free
	Tate Gallery	Mon–Sat 10am–5.50pm Sun 2–5.50pm	

❹ 📼 **Listen and check. Complete the** *When?* **and** *How much?* **columns in the chart.**

❺ **Complete the conversation with these sentences.**

a Four pounds fifty to eleven pounds.
b There's *A Midsummer Night's Dream* at the Open Air Theatre.
c At seven forty-five.

TESSA <u>What's</u> <u>on</u> at the <u>theatre</u> this <u>evening</u>?

MIKE   ....
       ....

TESSA Oh, I'd like to see that. <u>What</u> <u>time</u> does it <u>start</u>?

MIKE   ....
       ....

TESSA And <u>how</u> <u>much</u> does it <u>cost</u>?

MIKE   ....
       ....

📼 **Listen and check.**

❻ 📼 **Listen and repeat the questions in activity 5.**

C

D

❼ Ask and answer questions about the events in the chart.

What's on at the Tate Gallery today/tomorrow?
What's on at the Riverside Studios Cinema on Friday?

What time does the concert start/finish?
When does the gallery open/close?

How much does it cost?

Use the conversation in activity 5 to help you.

❽ Work in groups of four. Find out what's on in your town.

Now talk to other groups. Ask and answer questions about what's on in your town.

❾ Write sentences about four events in your town.

*There's a Franco
Battiato concert at
the Teatro Orfeo tonight.
It costs 20.000 lire.*

❿ Read the sentences. Put them in order and make a conversation. Start with sentence d.

a £16. And it starts at eight o'clock.
b I'm sorry, I can't. I'm busy on Friday.
c There's a Pink Floyd concert at Wembley Stadium.
d Would you like to go to a rock concert on Friday?
e Really? How much does it cost?
f Yes, I'd love to. What's on?
g That's fine. Where shall we meet?
h What about Saturday?

▄▄ **Listen and check.**

⓫ Invite other students to go out with you on different days. Accept or refuse their invitations.

A Would you like to go to
{
the theatre
the cinema
a concert
an exhibition
}
on (day)?

B Yes, I'd love to. What's on? / I'm sorry, I'm busy.

Make arrangements with at least three people.

⓬ Write short notes about your arrangements.

> Dear Juan,
>   The film starts at 7.30 on Saturday and it costs £5. Would you like to meet outside the cinema at 7 o'clock? Then we can go for a drink.
>   Best wishes,
>   Paulette

⓭ Find out where you can see English language films or plays. Invite other students for an English evening at the cinema/theatre.

Listen to people speaking English as often as you can.

In this lesson you practise:
● **Asking and saying how often**
● **Asking and saying what's on**
● **Asking and saying when things happen**
● **Asking and saying how much things cost (2)**
● **Making, accepting and refusing invitations (1)**
● **Prepositions of time:** *at, on*
● **Prepositions of place:** *at, to*
Now turn to page 52 and look at the STRUCTURES TO LEARN **and the** WORDS TO REMEMBER.

❶ Look at the title of the LIFESTYLE article. Which of these words do you expect to find in the article?

cupboard   bus   train
soldier   taxi   library   sea
vegetable   airport   tennis

Now read the article and check.

❷ Read the article again and decide where these sentences go.

a They arrive at San Francisco International or Oakland International Airports.
b Take one to the top of Nob Hill.
c However, you can take a boat from Fisherman's Wharf or Pier 39, and visit the bridge.

❸ Ask and say what people in the LIFESTYLE pictures are doing. Choose from these phrases.

listening to a concert
shopping   taking a boat trip
looking at paintings
sitting in a park   having lunch
looking at buildings
taking a cable car ride

A Are they listening to a concert?
B Yes, they are.

A Is the man looking at paintings?
B No, he isn't.

A What's the woman doing?
B She's having lunch.

❹ 🔲 **Listen and read.**

MAN   Ex<u>cuse</u> me. Can you <u>tell</u> me the <u>way</u> to the <u>Civic Center</u>?
WOMAN   <u>Yes</u>, <u>go</u> along <u>Geary</u> Street, turn <u>left</u> into <u>Polk</u> Street, and it's <u>straight</u> <u>ahead</u>.
MAN   And <u>how</u> do I <u>get</u> to <u>Nob Hill</u>?
WOMAN   <u>Go</u> along <u>Powell</u> Street, and it's on the <u>left</u>.
MAN   Thank <u>you</u>.

Now listen again and repeat.

Lifestyle on holiday i[n]

Getting there ar

So you're having a holiday in San Francisco? A very special way to come to San Francisco is by sea. B[?] these days few visitors arrive by bo[at] from the Pacific, pass through The Golden Gate, and go under the famous Bridge. 1. .... The m[?] popular boat trip is to Alcatraz with [?] two-hour guided tour of the former prison.

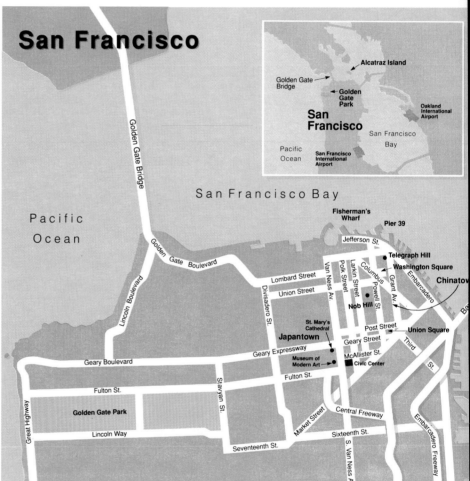

San Francisco

an Francisco

etting around

Most people come by air.
.... There is a 24-hour bus
ervice between the airports and the
r terminal near Union Square.
axis are good but very expensive.
The Bay Area Rapid Transit
BART) is a train service between
an Francisco and the East Bay,
nd stops at several stations,
uch as Oakland and Berkeley.
The Muni is the San Francisco
lunicipal Railway system with
uses, trams and trolley buses to
l districts of downtown San
rancisco. But it also runs the
able cars which run up and down
an Francisco's steep hills and are
ne of its most famous tourist
ttractions. 3. .... You get
e best view of this beautiful city
om here.

❺ You are in Union Square. Look at the map and answer the two
questions. Give directions using the sentences below in the correct
order.

> Excuse me, how do I get to Chinatown?

> Excuse me, can you tell me the way to Telegraph Hill?

a Turn left into Grant Avenue.
b Go along Powell Street to
Washington Square.

c It's straight ahead.
d Go along Post Street.
e It's on the right.

▪▪ **Listen and check.**

❻ **Ask for and give directions to these places.**

The Golden Gate Bridge   Golden Gate Park   Washington Square
Nob Hill   Chinatown   Japantown   The Civic Center
Museum of Modern Art   St Mary's Cathedral
Fisherman's Wharf   Pier 39

take the bus/train/cable car . . .

❼ **Say how you get to your town and how you get around it.**

❽ **Read this letter from a friend.**

> Dear ....,
> I'd like to come and see you
> next Saturday. How do I get from the
> station to your house?
> Please write soon.
>   Best wishes,
>   Chris

Now reply giving directions from the nearest station to your home.

❾ **Find some tourist information (in English) about the USA.**

1 How many place names do you recognise?
2 How many words do you understand?
3 Find three interesting/useful pieces of information.

In this lesson you practise:
● **Asking and saying what's happening**
● **The present continuous tense**
● **Asking for and giving directions**
● **Prepositions of place:** *in, into, along, over, on*
Now turn to page 53 and look at the STRUCTURES TO LEARN and the
WORDS TO REMEMBER.

What do your clothes say about you?

A 'There's a kind of uniform that goes with my job. I have to wear a suit, a white shirt and a tie in the office. I always carry a raincoat, and an umbrella – because of the weather in this country. I spend a lot of money on my clothes, but they last a long time.'

B 'I don't have much money, so all my clothes are second hand. I buy them from Oxfam. And I need practical clothes because I paint, and I cycle to college. I wear jeans and Doc Marten boots most of the time. I've got a lot of T-shirts and I usually wear my brother's leather jacket. Do you like my hat?'

Laura

Andy

❶ **Look at the pictures in** WHAT DO YOUR CLOTHES SAY ABOUT YOU? **What do you think the people do? Match the people with the jobs.**

a shop assistant   a teacher   an art student   an accountant

❷ **Read the paragraphs quickly and match them with the people.**

❸ **Read the paragraphs again and find the words for clothes and footwear.**

Ask and say the names of the items in the pictures.

A What's this?   A What are these?
B It's a shirt.   B Jeans.

❹ **Match the two parts of the sentences.**

1 James wears a suit in the office . . .
2 He always carries an umbrella . . .
3 All Laura's clothes are second hand . . .
4 She needs practical clothes . . .

a . . . because she doesn't have much money.
b . . . because it goes with the job.
c . . . because of the weather.
d . . . because she paints, and she cycles to college.

Now answer these questions.

1 Why does Margaret buy classic clothes?
2 Why does she wear a dress or skirt at school?
3 Why does Andy need to look smart?
4 Why does he always wear trainers?

❺ **Ask and say what clothes you wear in these situations and why.**

at school/work   at home   at a party

❻ 🔲 **Listen and read. Match the description with the person.**

CHRIS   That girl looks interesting.
DIANA   Which one? What's she wearing?
CHRIS   She's wearing a jacket and jeans.
DIANA   What colour's her jacket?
CHRIS   Black.
DIANA   And what colour are her jeans?
CHRIS   Blue. And she's wearing a hat.

red

white

green

blue

yellow   black

grey

brown   orange

C 'I haven't got the time or the money to buy lots of clothes, so I buy classic clothes. They're quite expensive but they last for years. This coat is ten years old. I can't wear trousers at school, so I wear a dress or a skirt and pullover. Most of my clothes are simple colours, black, blue or beige, but I often wear bright coloured tights – like red or green.'

D 'I need to look smart because of the customers. I buy lots of clothes because I get a discount from the shop. I wear a jacket and trousers and a shirt, but I never wear a tie. I like casual clothes and comfortable shoes – I always wear trainers.'

What kind of clothes do you wear?

James

Margaret

7 🔲 **Listen and repeat.**

<u>What</u>'s she <u>wearing</u>?
She's wearing a <u>jacket</u> and <u>jeans</u>.
<u>What</u> <u>colour</u>'s her <u>jacket</u>?
<u>What</u> <u>colour</u> are her <u>jeans</u>?

8 **Say what the people in the other pictures are wearing.**

He's wearing white trousers, an orange shirt . . .

9 **Work in pairs.**

STUDENT A   Choose someone in the class. Don't say who the person is. Talk about his/her clothes.

STUDENT B   Ask questions and find out who Student A is describing.

What's he/she wearing?

What colour is her jacket?
What colour is it?

What colour are his trousers?
What colour are they?

10 🔲 **Listen and tick the sentences you hear. They are in the right order. Then write the conversation.**

a   I'd like grey ones.
b   Good afternoon, sir. Can I help you?
c   They're £39.95.
d   Yes, I'm looking for a pullover.
e   Good morning, madam. Can I help you?
f   What colour would you like?
g   Green.
h   I'm afraid we haven't got any grey trousers. How about black?
i   Green? Yes, here you are.
j   No, I don't think so.
k   Yes, I'm looking for some trousers.
l   How much is it?
m   How much do they cost?
n   £14.95.
o   What colour do you want?
p   That's fine. Yes, I'll take it.

11 **Put the other sentences in the right order. Write the second conversation.**

🔲 **Now listen and check.**

12 **Work in pairs. Student A is a shop assistant. Student B is a customer. Act out the two conversations.**

Then act out other conversations in clothes/shoe shops.

13 **Look at the labels on your clothes. Can you find some English words?**

In this lesson you practise:
● **Asking for and giving reasons (1)**
● **Asking and saying what people are wearing**
● **Saying what you want to buy**
● **Asking and saying how much things cost (3)**
● **The present simple and present continuous**
Now turn to page 54 and look at the STRUCTURES TO LEARN and the WORDS TO REMEMBER.

1 Look at the photos in WHAT DO THESE PEOPLE HAVE IN COMMON? What do the people do? Choose from these words.

musician   pilot
businessman/woman   doctor
scientist   politician

She's a politician.

2 Ask and say what the people in the photos are doing. Choose from these phrases.

listening to instructions
reading a book   making a speech
singing a song   writing a letter
talking to a patient

What's the politician doing?

3 Read WHAT DO THESE PEOPLE HAVE IN COMMON? How many people speak English?

Match the jobs in activity 1 with the occupational fields in the article.

doctor – medicine

Think of other jobs where you need to speak English.

4 ▭ Listen and find out why these students are learning English. Tick the chart.

WHAT DO THESE PEOPLE HAVE IN COMMON?

They're all using English to communicate. About 300 million people speak English as a first language. More than one thousand million people speak English as a second or foreign language. In other words, about a third of the population of the world speaks English. It is the international language of medicine and science, politics and business, pop music and air travel. English is everywhere – in newspapers and films, on radio and television, at airports and hotels, on packets of food and bottles of medicine. It is the *lingua franca* of the world.

	Marie-Louise	Yassin	Celina
read books in English			
understand English films			
study medicine			
understand pop songs			
get a better job			
travel			
talk to people who don't speak my language			
go to America			
be an English teacher			

5 Ask and say why the three students are learning English.

A Why is Marie-Louise learning English?
B Because she'd like to . . . /Because she wants to . . .

Now ask and say why you are learning English.

6 ▭ Work in pairs. Listen to a man talking about his house.

STUDENT A   Listen for details of the rooms.
STUDENT B   Listen for details of the furniture.

Now try to remember all the details.

Has he got a . . . ?
Has it got a . . . ?
Is there a . . . ?
How many . . . are there?

Write a description of the house with your partner.

7 Say which of these activities you associate with free time.

getting up   skiing   listening to the radio   going to work/school
singing and dancing   learning English   reading books and newspapers
swimming   watching or playing football   going to restaurants

8 Look at the photos. Where do you think these places are? What are the people doing?

Think of two more things which people in hot countries like doing, and two more things which people in cold countries like doing in their free time.

9 Work in pairs.

STUDENT A   Turn to page 110 for your instructions.
STUDENT B   Turn to page 112 for your instructions.

10 Say what people in your country like doing in their free time.

11 Write your diary for next week. Then invite other students to go out with you, and accept or refuse their invitations.

STUDENT A
– Invite Student B to go to a
  play/film/concert/exhibition
  with you on (*day*).
– Say what's on.
– Say how much it costs.
– Say when it starts.
– Suggest another time/day.
– Give directions.

STUDENT B
– Accept the invitation. Ask what's
  on.
– Ask how much it costs.
– Ask when it starts.
– Say you're busy at that time.
– Accept the invitation. Ask for
  directions.

Complete your diary with things to do for each day of the week.

12 Work in pairs.

STUDENT A   **You are a shop assistant. You sell five kinds of clothes in five different colours. Make a list of the clothes, their colours and their prices.**
STUDENT B   **You want to buy something new to wear. Decide what colour you want. Visit shops and try to find what you are looking for.**

13 Look at signs, advertisements, packets of food and bottles of medicine. Can you find some English words?

14 Read these letters.

ANY QUESTIONS?

WRITE TO THE LANGUAGE DOCTOR

QUESTION   In English, there are a lot of words like this: *I'd, he's, aren't, don't*. What do you call them? Is it correct to use these forms?
Yuri, Osaka

ANSWER   *I'd, he's, aren't* and *don't* are all contractions. I'm sure you know what the full forms are. When we speak, it's quite correct to use contractions. When we write letters to friends, we use them too. But we don't use contractions in business letters or scientific reports, for example.

Have you got any questions about English? Write a letter to the language doctor and give it to your teacher.

STRUCTURES TO LEARN

Asking and saying what people like and what people like doing

Do you like jazz?	Yes, I do. / Yes, I love it. It's all right. / Not very much. No, I don't.
Does he/she like swimming?	Yes, he/she does. Not very much. No, he/she doesn't.
What kind of music do you like?	I like samba *but* I don't like reggae.
What kind of music does he/she like?	He likes folk music *and* jazz. She doesn't like blues *or* disco.

	Same	Different
I like dancing. I don't like watching TV.	So do I. Nor do I.	Do you? I don't. Don't you? I do.

WORDS TO REMEMBER

music /mjuːzɪk/   blues /bluːz/   classical /klæsɪkəl/
country and western /kʌntri ən wɛstən/
disco /dɪskəʊ/   folk /fəʊk/   jazz /dʒæz/
opera /ɒprə/   reggae /rɛgeɪ/   rock /rɒk/
samba /sæmbə/

cook /kʊk/   dance /dɑːns/   go /gəʊ/
go out /gəʊ aʊt/   leave /liːv/   play /pleɪ/
run /rʌn/   sit /sɪt/   stay /steɪ/   swim /swɪm/
watch /wɒtʃ/

cinema /sɪnəmə/   concert /kɒnsət/
football /fʊtbɔːl/   friend /frɛnd/   letter /lɛtə/
party /pɑːti/   TV /tiːviː/   tennis /tɛnɪs/
theatre /θɪətə/

PRACTICE EXERCISES

❶ 🔊 **Answer the questions.**

Example: *Do you like jazz?*
   Yes, I do. or No, I don't.
   or Not very much.

1 jazz
2 reading
3 cooking
4 opera
5 country and western music
6 playing tennis

❷ **Write *do, don't, does* or *doesn't*.**

1 What kind of music . . . you like?
2 – . . . he like jazz?
   – No, he . . . .
3 – Steve . . . like football.
   – Nor . . . I.
4 – . . . they like going to the cinema?
   – Yes, they . . . .
5 – We like singing, but we . . . like dancing.
   – Nor . . . we.
6 She . . . like disco music, but I . . . .

🔊 **Listen and check.**

❸ 🔊 **Listen and repeat.**

1 Do you like rock music?

2 Does he like swimming?

3 What kind of music do you like?

4 She likes dancing, going to the cinema and

   watching television.

Now read the sentences aloud.

❹ 🔊 **Ask questions. Listen to the answers and put a tick or a cross.**

Example: *Jack likes playing football.*
   Does he like swimming?
   Yes, he does.

1 Jack likes playing football. (swimming) ✓
2 Lucy likes classical music. (opera)
3 Helen doesn't like dancing. (going to parties)
4 Steve doesn't like folk music. (blues)
5 My children like disco music. (rock music)
6 My mother and father don't like watching TV. (going to the cinema)

❺ 🔊 **Answer the questions. Use the answers in exercise 4.**

Example: *Does Jack like swimming?*
   Yes, he does.

❻ **Look at the answers in exercise 4. Write sentences.**

Example: 1 *Jack likes playing football and swimming.*

🔊 **Listen and check.**

STRUCTURES TO LEARN

Talking about people's homes

Do	you they he	live in a house?	Yes,	I they he she	do. does.
Does	she		No,	I they he she	don't. doesn't.

For more information about the question form in the present simple tense, see *Lesson 10 LANGUAGE STUDY*.

Questions	Short answers
Has it got a dining room?	Yes, it has. No, it hasn't.
Is there a garden?	Yes, there is. No, there isn't.
How many rooms has it got? are there?	

Present tense: *have got*

Affirmative

Full form	Short form
I have got	I've got
you have got	you've got
he/she/it has got	he's/she's/it's got
we have got	we've got
they have got	they've got

Negative

Full form	Short form
I have not got	I haven't got
you have not got	you haven't got
he/she/it has not got	he/she/it hasn't got
we have not got	we haven't got
they have not got	they haven't got

Questions

Have I got . . . ?
Have you got . . . ?
Has he/she/it got . . . ?
Have we got . . . ?
Have they got . . . ?

WORDS TO REMEMBER

flat /flæt/   house /haʊs/   upstairs /ʌpstɛəz/ downstairs /daʊnstɛəz/

bathroom /bɑːθruːm/   bedroom /bɛdruːm/ dining room /daɪnɪŋ ruːm/   garden /gɑːdən/ kitchen /kɪtʃɪn/   sitting room /sɪtɪŋ ruːm/ toilet /tɔɪlɪt/

armchair /ɑːmtʃɛə/   basin /beɪsən/   bath /bɑːθ/ chair /tʃɛə/   cooker /kʊkə/   cupboard /kʌbəd/ door /dɔː/   fridge /frɪdʒ/   shower /ʃaʊə/ sink /sɪŋk/   sofa /səʊfə/   stairs /stɛəz/ table /teɪbəl/   television /tɛlɪvɪʒən/ wardrobe /wɔːdrəʊb/   window /wɪndəʊ/

pronounce /prənaʊns/

PRACTICE EXERCISES

❶ **Underline the stressed syllables.**

upstairs   downstairs   bathroom   bedroom garden   kitchen   toilet   armchair   cooker cupboard   shower   sofa   table   television

▭ **Listen and check. Repeat the words.**

❷ ▭ **Ask questions. Listen to the answers and put a tick or a cross.**

Example: *John*
       Does John live in a house?
       No, he doesn't. He lives in a flat.

1 John/house ✗
2 Steve and Mary/house
3 Jenny/flat
4 Lucy and her husband/flat
5 John's sister/house
6 Pat's father/flat

❸ **Look at the answers in exercise 2. Write sentences.**

Example: 1 *John doesn't live in a house. He lives in a flat.*

▭ **Listen and check.**

❹ ▭ **Answer questions about John's flat.**

Example: Has it got a dining room?
       No, it hasn't.

1 a dining room? ✗   4 a garden? ✗
2 a bathroom? ✓   5 two bedrooms? ✓
3 a kitchen? ✓   6 a sitting room? ✓

STRUCTURES TO LEARN

Asking and saying how often

How often do you go to the cinema?	Once a week. Twice a month. Three times a year. I never go to the cinema.

Asking and saying what's on

What's on at the theatre	this evening? today? on Monday?	There's Macbeth at the Apollo.

Asking and saying when things happen

When does it start? What time does it open/close?	At seven thirty. At 10 a.m.

Asking and saying how much things cost (2)

How much does it cost?	Three pounds fifty. It's free.

Making, accepting and refusing invitations (1)

Would you like to go to the cinema?	Yes, I'd love to. I'm sorry, I can't. I'm busy.

Prepositions of time: *at, on*

at seven-thirty   *on* Monday
at twenty to twelve   *on* Friday
at the weekend   *on* Sunday

For more prepositions of time, see Lessons 10, 17 and 19 *LANGUAGE STUDY*.

Prepositions of place: *at, to*

There's an exhibition *at* the gallery. What's on this week *at* the theatre?	Would you like to go *to* the theatre? How often do you go *to* the cinema?

For more prepositions of place, see *Lessons 2, 14* and *16 LANGUAGE STUDY*.

WORDS TO REMEMBER

exhibition /ɛgzɪbɪʃən/   film /fɪlm/
gallery /gæləri/   play /pleɪ/

today /tədeɪ/   tomorrow /təmɒrəʊ/
month /mʌnθ/   week /wiːk/   year /jɪə/

cost /kɒst/

never /nɛvə/   once /wʌns/   twice /twaɪs/
three times /θriː taɪmz/

PRACTICE EXERCISES

1 📼 **Listen and underline the stressed words.**
1 How often do you go to the theatre?
2 What time does the film finish?
3 What's on at the theatre this evening?
4 How much does it cost?
5 Would you like to go to the cinema?

Now read the sentences aloud.

2 **Write *at*, *on* or *in*.**
1 The film starts . . . five o'clock.
2 Would you like to go to the theatre . . . Monday?
3 The pubs close . . . eleven o'clock.
4 The restaurant is closed . . . Sunday evening and . . . Monday . . . lunchtime.
5 The gallery opens . . . two . . . the afternoon.

📼 **Listen and check.**

3 📼 **Ask questions. Listen and write the times.**

Example: *film/start*
          What time does the film start?
          It starts at ten to eight.

1 film/start	7.50	4 lessons/start	
2 gallery/open		5 restaurant/open	
3 play/start		6 pubs/close	

4 **Look at the answers in exercise 3. Write sentences.**

Example: 1 *The film starts at ten to eight.*

5 📼 **Answer the questions.**

Example: *How much does the cinema ticket cost?*
          Two pounds twenty-five.

1 cinema ticket £2.25	4 TV £175
2 hotel £30	5 theatre ticket £7.80
3 exhibition £4	6 football match £5.90

6 **Complete the dialogue.**
A Would . . . like to go . . . the cinema this evening?
B I' . . . sorry, I can't. I'm busy.
A Well, . . . you like to go on Thursday?
B Yes, I'd love . . . . What's on?
A There's a Hitchcock film . . . the Odeon Cinema.
B . . . much does . . . cost?
A Three . . . fifty. And it starts . . . half . . . seven.
B Great! See you . . . Thursday.

Underline the important words.

📼 **Now listen and check. The stressed words are the most important words.**

STRUCTURES TO LEARN

Asking and saying what's happening

Present continuous tense

You use the present continuous tense to talk about what's happening at the moment.

You're looking at Lesson 14 at the moment.
You're learning English.

Affirmative short forms	Negative short forms
I'm visiting	I'm not visiting
you're visiting	you aren't visiting
he's/she's visiting	he/she isn't visiting
we're/they're visiting	we/they aren't visiting

Questions

Am I visiting?	Is he/she visiting?
Are you/we/they visiting?	

Short answers

Yes, I am.	No, I'm not.
Yes, you/we/they are.	No, you/we/they/aren't.
Yes, he/she is.	No, he/she isn't.

Verbs which end in -*e* drop this ending and add -*ing*.
  have having   close closing
Verbs of one syllable which end in a vowel and a consonant double the consonant and add -*ing*.
  shop shopping   get getting
But verbs of one syllable which end in a vowel and -*y* or -*w* add -*ing*.
  play playing   stay staying

For more information about the present continuous, see *Lesson 15 LANGUAGE STUDY*.

Asking for and giving directions

Excuse me, how do I get to the post office? Excuse me, can you tell me the way to Chinatown?	Go along the street. Go over the bridge. Cross the road. Turn left into the High Street.

Prepositions of place: *in, into*
  He lives *in* San Francisco.
  Turn right *into* Union Street.

along, over   *on*
  Go *along* Powell Street.   It's *on* the left.
  Go *over* the Golden Gate Bridge. It's *on* the right.

For more prepositions of place, see *Lessons 2, 13 and 16 LANGUAGE STUDY*.

WORDS TO REMEMBER

look /lʊk/ take /teɪk/ visit /vɪzɪt/ cross /krɒs/
tell /tɛl/ turn /tɜ:n/

air /ɛə/ airport /ɛəpɔ:t/ cable car /keɪbəl kɑ:/
boat /bəʊt/ bus /bʌs/ sea /si:/ station /steɪʃən/
taxi /tæksi/ train /treɪn/ tram /træm/

bridge /brɪdʒ/ building /bɪldɪŋ/ hill /hɪl/
park /pɑ:k/ road /rəʊd/ square /skwɛə/
street /stri:t/

in the middle /ɪn ðə mɪdəl/
on the left /ɒn ðə lɛft/ on the right /ɒn ðə raɪt/

PRACTICE EXERCISES

❶ Underline the most important words.

1 Ex<u>cuse</u> me, how do I get to <u>China</u>town?
2 Can you tell me the way to the Civic Center?
3 Go along Powell Street and it's on the left.
4 Turn right into Bay Street and it's straight ahead.

▭▭ **Listen and check. The stressed words are the most important words.**

❷ Write *in*, *into*, *along*, *over* or *on*.

1 Go . . . Columbus Avenue.
2 Turn right . . . Powell Street.
3 It's pleasant to sit . . . Golden Gate Park.
4 The Civic Center is . . . the left.
5 Go . . . the Golden Gate Bridge.

▭▭ **Listen and check.**

❸ ▭▭ Ask how to get to places. Use *How do I get to . . .?*

Example: *Nob Hill*
       Excuse me, how do I get to Nob Hill?

1 Nob Hill	4 the air terminal
2 the station	5 the Museum of Modern Art
3 Telegraph Hill	6 Golden Gate Park

❹ ▭▭ Ask the way to the places in exercise 3. Use *Can you tell me the way to . . .?*

Example: *Nob Hill*
       Excuse me, can you tell me the way to Nob Hill?

❺ ▭▭ Answer the questions and say what people are doing.

Example: *What's James doing?*
       He's listening to a concert.

1 James/listen to a concert
2 Maria/shopping
3 Sophie and George/taking a boat trip
4 Henry/having dinner
5 Sheila and Margaret/looking at paintings

STRUCTURES TO LEARN

Asking for and giving reasons (1)
Why does he wear a suit?
Because it goes with the job.

See also *Lesson 18 LANGUAGE STUDY.*

Asking and saying what people are wearing

What's he/she wearing?	He/She's wearing a suit.

What colour is	her jacket? it?	It's green.
What colour are	his trousers? they?	They're brown.

Saying what you want to buy

I'm looking for I want I'd like	a jacket. some jeans.

Asking how much things cost (3)

How much	is it? does it cost?	How much	are they? do they cost?

Present simple or present continuous
You use the present simple to talk about a permanent state or a routine action/event.
  I like dancing.
  He gets up at seven o'clock.

You use the present continuous to talk about something that is happening at the moment.
  Can I help you?
  Yes, I'm looking for some clothes.

Here we are in San Francisco and we're having lunch on Fisherman's Wharf.

WORDS TO REMEMBER

buy /baɪ/   carry /kæri/   want /wɒnt/   wear /wɛə/

clothes /kləʊðz/   coat /kəʊt/   boot /buːt/
hat /hæt/   jacket /dʒækɪt/   jeans /dʒiːnz/
pullover /pʊləʊvə/   raincoat /reɪnkəʊt/
shirt /ʃɜːt/   skirt /skɜːt/   suit /suːt/   tie /taɪ/
tights /taɪts/   trainers /treɪnəz/   trousers /traʊzəz/
umbrella /ʌmbrɛlə/

colour /kʌlə/   black /blæk/   blue /bluː/
brown /braʊn/   green /griːn/   grey /greɪ/
orange /ɒrɪndʒ/   red /rɛd/   white /waɪt/
yellow /jɛləʊ/

always /ɔːlwɪz/

PRACTICE EXERCISES

❶ ▭ Listen and repeat. Make sure your voice rises and falls with the arrows.

1 Can I help you?

2 Yes, I'm looking for a pullover.

3 Why do you always wear a suit?

4 Because it goes with the job.

5 What's she wearing?

6 She's wearing a jacket, jeans and trainers.

Now read the sentences aloud.

❷ ▭ Ask questions.

Example: *She always wears trousers.*
         Why does she always wear trousers?

1 She always wears trousers.
2 They always carry umbrellas.
3 He always buys red ties.
4 They always wear hats.
5 She always buys black clothes.
6 He always wears a raincoat.

❸ ▭ Ask how much things cost. Listen and write the prices.

Example: *trousers*
         How much do the trousers cost?
         Twenty-nine pounds.

1 trousers £29	3 jeans	5 raincoat
2 jacket	4 shoes	6 shirt

❹ Complete the sentences with the present simple or present continuous form of the verbs in brackets.

1 I . . . a new suit because I . . . to look smart for my job. (buy, need)
2 – Where's David?
   – He . . . his parents. (visit)
3 Why . . . you . . . a tie this evening? (wear)
4 He always . . . second-hand clothes. (buy)
5 . . . you . . . pizza? (like)
6 – What . . . you . . .? (do)
   – I . . . television. (watch)

▭ Listen and check.

Panorama

4

Britain in view: Behind the scenes
On tour with a theatre company
Take three travellers: what to take when you travel
Beyond the Blue Horizon: The first passenger flights
   from Britain to Australia
Bob Geldof and Live Aid
PLUS
The story of Beryl Markham - a pioneer of the 20th century

behind

Britain in view

the scenes

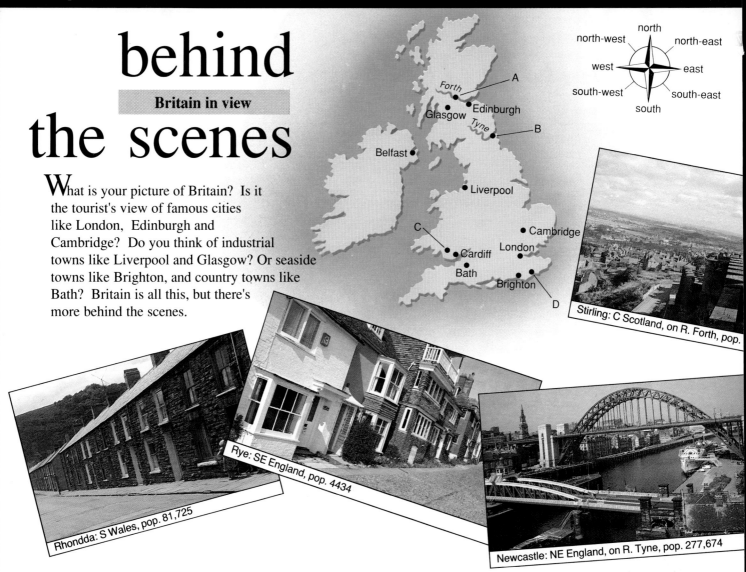

What is your picture of Britain? Is it the tourist's view of famous cities like London, Edinburgh and Cambridge? Do you think of industrial towns like Liverpool and Glasgow? Or seaside towns like Brighton, and country towns like Bath? Britain is all this, but there's more behind the scenes.

north
north-west   north-east
west   east
south-west   south-east
south

Stirling: C Scotland, on R. Forth, pop.

Rye: SE England, pop. 4434

Rhondda: S Wales, pop. 81,725

Newcastle: NE England, on R. Tyne, pop. 277,674

❶ Read BRITAIN IN VIEW and look at the photos. What is your picture of Britain?

❷ Match the photos with the letters on the map of Britain.

❸ 📼 Listen and repeat.

A Where's Stirling?
B It's in the middle of Scotland.
   It's on the River Forth.

Now ask and say where the other places in the photos are.

	in the north/south/east/west.
It's	in the centre/middle.
	on the coast.
	on the River (name).

❹ Ask and say where these towns and cities are.

Granada Paris Calcutta Perth Mombasa Santiago Odessa
Birmingham Madrid Recife Vienna Milan Helsinki

❺ These cities are all capital cities. Find their countries and complete the puzzle.

Ankara Beijing Berne
Bucharest Cairo Montevideo
Muscat New Delhi Oslo

Beijing is the capital of China.

	Population
C H I N A	1,059,521,000
O _ _ _	1,500,000
U _ _ _ _ _	3,012,000
N _ _ _ _ _	4,159,335
T _ _ _ _ _	51,428,514
R _ _ _ _ _	23,017,000
I _ _ _ _	750,900,000
E _ _ _ _	49,000,000
S _ _ _ _ _ _ _ _ _	6,484,800

❻ Ask and say.

A What's the capital of China?
B Beijing.
A And what's the population of China?
B One thousand and fifty-nine million, five hundred and twenty-one thousand. / About one thousand million.

What's the capital of your country? What's the population?

7 Look at the photographs. Do you know the names of the towns and/or the countries?

▣▣ Listen to people talking about these towns. Match the photographs with the descriptions.

Listen again and write down the name of each place, the population, and the country.

8 Ask and say what the places in activity 7 are like. Use these words and phrases.

a (very) ⎫
(quite) a ⎭ big/small town/city/village/port

in the north/south/east/west (of . . .)
on the coast/River (name)
in the mountains

a(n) commercial/industrial town/city
a tourist centre

(quite/very) interesting/pretty/beautiful/old/modern/
   busy/crowded/quiet/noisy/dangerous

A   What's Bangkok like?
B   It's a very big city in the south of Thailand. It's got a population of about five and a half million people. It's the capital of Thailand and it's a commercial and industrial city. It's also a busy port. It's very interesting but it's quite dangerous.

9 Work in pairs. Ask what your partner's town is like. Say what your town is like.

10 Write a description of the place you are in at the moment.

11 Ask and say where you would like to go in the world. Why?

12 In the dictionary, words are listed with their parts of speech. For example:

river *n* (*noun*)   write *v* (*verb*)
pretty *adj* (*adjective*)
on *prep* (*preposition*)

Find four nouns, four verbs, four adjectives, and four prepositions in this lesson. Then check the words in a dictionary.

> In this lesson you practise:
> ● Describing places
> ● Prepositions of place: *in, on*
> Now turn to page 68 and look at the STRUCTURES TO LEARN and the WORDS TO REMEMBER.

ON TOUR WITH
Cheek by Jowl

Cheek by Jowl is a touring theatre company. Since the first performance of *The Country Wife* at the Edinburgh Festival in 1981, the company has performed across five continents in over 250 towns. Next week the actors are going on tour again. This time it's Europe, with *The Tempest* by William Shakespeare and *Philoctetes* by Sophocles.

❶ Read ON TOUR WITH CHEEK BY JOWL and look at the photo. Find out what *Cheek by Jowl* is.

❷ 🔲 Listen to the first part of an interview with Timothy Walker, one of the actors in *Cheek by Jowl*. Tick the countries the company is visiting.

Sweden   Romania   Hungary   Norway   Italy   Turkey
Czechoslovakia   Greece   Poland

Now complete the chart with the countries in the right order.

date	country	city	number of performances
6 March			
13 March			
27 March			
3 April			

❸ Match the cities with the countries in activity 2.

Prague   Bucharest   Ankara
Oslo   Istanbul   Bratislava

🔲 Listen again and check. Then complete the *city* column in the chart.

❹ 🔲 Listen to the second part of the interview and write the number of performances in each city.

5 ■■ **Listen and repeat the dates.**

you write	you say
6th March	the <u>sixth</u> of <u>March</u> *or* <u>March</u> the <u>sixth</u>
13th March	the <u>thirteenth</u> of <u>March</u> *or* <u>March</u> the <u>thirteenth</u>
20th March	the <u>twentieth</u> of <u>March</u> *or* <u>March</u> the <u>twentieth</u>
27th March	the <u>twenty-seventh</u> of <u>March</u> *or* <u>March</u> the <u>twenty-seventh</u>
3rd April	the <u>third</u> of <u>April</u> *or* <u>April</u> the <u>third</u>

6 **Ask and answer questions about the *Cheek by Jowl* tour.**

Which countries are the actors visiting?
When are they going to . . . ?
How many performances are they doing in . . . ?
Where are they going after that?
When are they flying home?

7 **Complete the itinerary for the *Cheek by Jowl* tour.**

The actors are leaving Britain on 6th March. First they are flying to Norway and doing five performances in Oslo. Then they are going to . . . . They are doing . . . performances in . . . and . . . . After that they are . . . to . . . and they are . . . . . . performances in . . . . Finally they . . . . . . to . . . , where they . . . . performances in . . . and . . . . They . . . flying home on . . . April.

8 **Match the ordinal numbers.**

1st 2nd 3rd 4th 5th 6th 7th 8th 9th 10th 11th 12th

fourth tenth first sixth twelfth second ninth third
eleventh seventh fifth eighth

9 **Write the months of the year in the correct order.**

April November June January September March August
December February July October May

■■ **Listen and check. Repeat the months and mark the stress.**

10 **Ask and say.**

A What's the first/second/third month of the year? (etc.)
B It's . . .

A What's the date today/ tomorrow?
B It's . . .

A What was the date yesterday?
B It was . . .

11 **Make a class birthday chart. Say when your birthday is. Listen and write the other students' birthdays.**

A When's your birthday, Roberto?
B It's (on) July the thirtieth.
A Katja, what about you?
C My birthday's (on) the twenty-third of May.

Say *Happy birthday* to people on their birthday.

12 **Think about your arrangements. What are you doing next week/month? Look at your diary and write a list of dates when you are busy.**

Now work in pairs. Give your list of dates to your partner. Ask about the dates on your partner's list and answer his/her questions.

A What are you doing on September the nineteenth?
B I'm getting married!

13 **Write sentences about your partner's arrangements.**

Stefan is going to the doctor on 2nd April. He's going on holiday on 14th June. He's going to Canada with his brother. They're flying to Montreal.

14 **Write the ordinal numbers from 13th–31st. You can find some of the numbers in this lesson.**

13th — thirteenth
14th — fourteenth
15th — fifteenth

Use a dictionary to check the spelling.

15 **Try to keep your diary of appointments and arrangements in English.**

In this lesson you practise:
● Talking about the future (1): Arrangements
● Question words
● Asking and saying the date
● Prepositions of time: *on*, *in*
Now turn to page 69 and look at the STRUCTURES TO LEARN and the WORDS TO REMEMBER.

1 Read the descriptions of climate. Match them with the places below.

Denmark   Kenya
Tennessee, USA   Italy
Argentina   Singapore

> ### CLIMATE
> **tropical:** hot, wet summers, warm, dry winters – Central America, India, E Africa
> **tropical wet:** hot and wet all year – tropical rainforests of the Amazon and SE Asia
> **warm humid:** warm all year, regular rain – SE USA, S China
> **warm dry:** warm, dry summers, cool, wet winters – Mediterranean countries
> **cool humid:** cool summers, cold winters, regular rain – N Europe
> **cool dry:** cool, dry summers, cold, dry winters – Russian steppes, NW USA, Argentina

2 🔲 Listen and read. The man is from one of the places in activity 1. Where is he from?

WOMAN   What's the weather like?
MAN   It's usually very hot in summer, and it's warm in winter.
WOMAN   Does it often rain?
MAN   It rains a lot in summer, but it doesn't often rain in winter.
WOMAN   Does it ever snow?
MAN   Well, it sometimes snows in the mountains.

Now listen again and repeat.

3 🔲 Listen to two more people from places in activity 1. Where are they from?

4 Ask and say.

What's the weather like in . . .?

5 Write sentences about the weather in your country.

Take three travellers

Three famous travellers talk about what they take with them when they go away.

Christina Dodwell has travelled for ten years, from the Sahara to Papua New Guinea. She's written four books: her latest is *A Traveller in China*. 'I don't take a lot for first aid. I always wear a long skirt. I always take a hammock, photos of my family and postcards of home. But I never take a gun.'

Michael Wood is a TV journalist. 'I take a Swiss Army knife, a safety razor, credit card, passport and a spare pair of jeans. I like to travel light.'

Eric Newby is a travel writer. 'I always wear hats. I take my Italian corkscrew everywhere. In moments of danger I rely on a little book called *Help! First Aid for Everyday Emergencies,* and a very loud whistle.'

6 Read TAKE THREE TRAVELLERS and match the paragraphs with the photos of the people.

7 The three people always travel with certain items. Write down the things they mention. Which of the items can you see in the photos?

8 Read the questions. What do you think the reasons are?

1 Why does Christina Dodwell always wear a long skirt?
2 Why does she take photos of her family, and postcards of home?
3 Why does she never take a gun?
4 Why does Michael Wood take a Swiss Army knife?
5 Why does Eric Newby always wear hats?
6 He takes a whistle in case of danger – what else does he use it for?

9 Find the travellers' reasons in the list below.

a 'mainly for pulling wine corks'
b 'for calling taxis'
c 'In a lot of places, life is cheap and guns are valuable.'
d 'You can show them to people and suddenly you're no longer a foreign devil.'
e 'because I'm bald'
f 'because if you dress well, people treat you well'

Now decide where these phrases and sentences go in TAKE THREE TRAVELLERS.

10 Here are some more things which people take when they travel. Which of these words do you know? Write down the words you aren't sure about or don't know.

pair of shorts   swimming costume   pullover   gloves   walking boots
scarf   water bottle   trainers   rucksack   map   sunglasses   camera
umbrella   phrase book   travellers' cheques   anorak   torch
warm socks   first aid kit   sleeping bag   keys   alarm clock

Now compare your list with another student. Can you help each other with some of these words?

11 Write down three things which you always take when you travel, and three things which you never take.

Now work in pairs. Tell your partner about the items on your list.

I always take a swimming costume, because lots of hotels have
  swimming pools.
I don't like camping so I never take a sleeping bag.

12 Work in pairs. You are going on holiday next month to one of the places in activity 1. Choose a camping or a hotel holiday. Think about the weather and choose ten items which you should take with you.

I think we should take . . . because . . .
It's hot/cold in . . . so we (don't) need to take . . .

Now ask other pairs/students what they are taking on holiday. Can you guess where they are going?

13 Read this letter.

> La Coruña
> 27th February
>
> Dear Patrice,
>   I'm very pleased
> you're coming to La Coruña
> in April. But it rains a
> lot, and it's not very
> warm here, so you should
> bring an umbrella and a
> pullover. You don't need
> to bring a swimming
> costume !
>
>   Best wishes,
>
>   Ignacio

Now write a letter to a friend who is coming to your town. Say what the weather is like, and what your friend should bring.

14 Make sure you understand all the WORDS TO REMEMBER. Decide which words are most useful to you. Choose *fifteen* words to learn. Talk to other students about the words they have chosen.

> In this lesson you practise:
> • Talking about the weather
> • Adverbs of frequency
> • Giving reasons (2)
> • Saying what is
>   necessary/advisable
> Now turn to page 70 and look
> at the STRUCTURES TO LEARN
> and the WORDS TO REMEMBER.

❶ Look at the cover of *Beyond the Blue Horizon* and at the map. What is the book about?

Now read the first paragraph of the book review and check.

❷ Work in pairs. Say where the places are on the Imperial Airways route.

Alexandria   Brindisi
Darwin   Delhi   Kuwait
Rangoon   Singapore

I think Kuwait is between Baghdad and Bahrain.

❸ Write words from the book review under these headings.

time	travel
a few hours	*fly*

❹ ▭ Two people are talking about the Imperial Airways journey. Listen and check your answers to activity 2.

❺ Read these sentences.

1 The first flight was in 1934.
2 The journey started at Croydon Airport, London.
3 The passengers went from Paris to Brindisi by train.
4 They flew from Alexandria to Cairo.
5 The journey finished in Melbourne.
6 It took two months.
7 The passengers stopped in over 30 places.
8 The passengers were comfortable on the plane.
9 The journey was tiring.
10 They travelled at night.
11 At night the plane landed.
12 They had dinner on the plane.
13 They stayed on the plane at night.
14 They left early in the morning.
15 They visited lots of interesting places.
16 It was a boring journey.

Book Review

BEYOND THE BLUE HORIZON
by Alexander Frater
(William Heinemann, 1986/
Penguin Books Ltd 1987)

Today you can fly almost anywhere in the world in a few hours. But until this century, most people travelled by boat. Some journeys took months at sea. Then in 1935, Imperial Airways started a passenger service from Britain to Australia. The journey took two weeks, but it was the start of long distance air travel. In *Beyond the Blue Horizon*, Alexander Frater describes the Imperial Airways journey from Britain to Australia as he takes the same route fifty years later.
   The result is an exciting and often extremely funny account of

▭ **Listen to the second part of the conversation. Decide if the sentences are true or false.**

❻ ▭ Listen and read.

A   Did the journey take a long time?
B   <u>Yes</u>, it <u>did</u>.
A   Were the passengers comfortable?
B   <u>Yes</u>, they <u>were</u>.
A   Was the journey tiring?
B   <u>No</u>, it <u>wasn't</u>.
A   Did the passengers stay on the plane at night?
B   <u>No</u>, they <u>didn't</u>.

Listen again and repeat the answers.

London
Paris

Athe

IMPERIAL AIRWAYS

❼ Look at the sentences in activity 5. Find the past tense form(s) of these verbs.

be   finish   fly   go   have
land   leave   start   stay
stop   take   travel   visit

Six of these verbs are irregular. Which ones are they?

❽ Ask and answer questions about the Imperial Airways service to Australia.

A   Was the first flight in 1934?
B   No, it wasn't.
A   Did the journey start at Croydon Airport?
B   Yes, it did.

❾ Answer the questions.

1 When was the first passenger flight from Britain to Australia?
2 How did the passengers travel from Alexandria to Cairo?
3 Where did the journey finish?
4 How long did the journey take?
5 What was the journey like?
6 What happened at night?

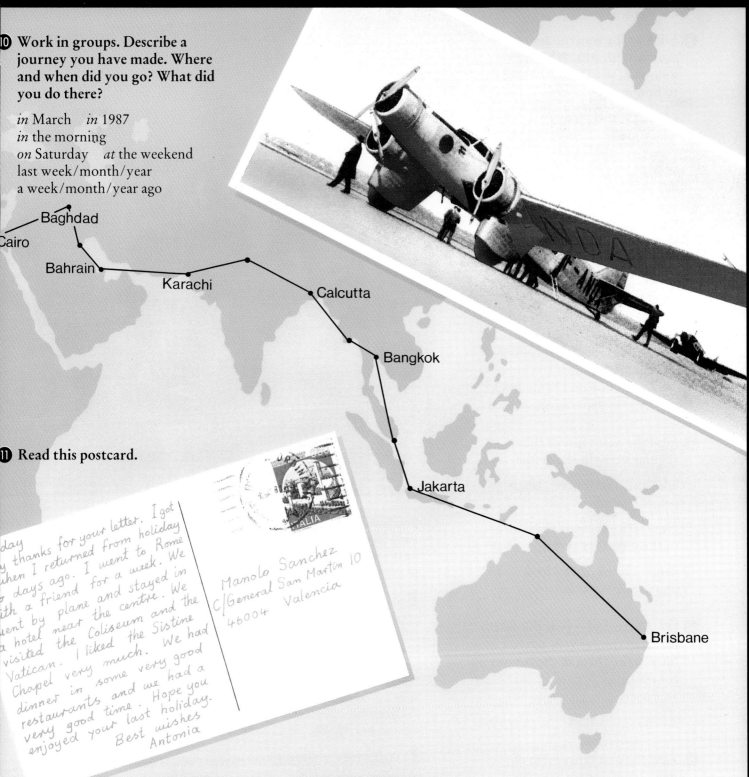

10 Work in groups. Describe a journey you have made. Where and when did you go? What did you do there?

in March   *in* 1987
in the morning
on Saturday   *at* the weekend
last week/month/year
a week/month/year ago

Baghdad
Cairo
Bahrain
Karachi
Calcutta
Bangkok
Jakarta
Brisbane

11 Read this postcard.

...day
...y thanks for your letter. I got
...when I returned from holiday
...o days ago. I went to Rome
...ith a friend for a week. We
...ent by plane and stayed in
...a hotel near the centre. We
...visited the Coliseum and the
...Vatican. I liked the Sistine
...Chapel very much. We had
...dinner in some very good
...restaurants and we had a
...very good time. Hope you
...enjoyed your last holiday.
          Best wishes
             Antonia

Manolo Sanchez
C/General San Martin 10
46004   Valencia

Now write a postcard to a friend. Describe your last holiday.

12 What do you say if you don't understand a question? What do you say if you don't know the answer? Practise these useful phrases, and use them if necessary!

(I'm sorry,) {
I don't understand.
I didn't hear that.
I don't know.
I'm not sure.
I can't remember.
}

In this lesson you practise:
- Talking about the past (1)
- Expressions of past time
- Prepositions of time: *in, at, on*

Now turn to page 71 and look at the STRUCTURES TO LEARN and the WORDS TO REMEMBER.

1 **Look at the BOB GELDOF AND LIVE AID photos. Which of the following words do you expect to find in the article?**

concert   river   record
Africa   snow   pop star
passport   famous   salad
doctor   TV

2 **Read the article and check. Choose a caption for each photo from this list.**

- In October 1984, Geldof saw the news about Ethiopia.
- On Sunday 25 November 1984, Band Aid recorded *Do They Know It's Christmas?*
- In December 1984, Geldof went to Ethiopia.
- At 12 noon on 13 July 1985, the Live Aid concert started.

3 **Find the past tense of these regular verbs in the article.**

ask   call   continue   decide
record   want   work

Now write the past tense form of these regular verbs.

dance   listen   live   look
play   talk   watch

4 🔲 **Listen and repeat the past forms of the verbs in activity 3. Now write them in the correct columns.**

/t/	/d/	/ɪd/
asked	called	decided

5 **Find the past tense form of these irregular verbs in the article.**

become   begin   choose
come   go   make   see   sell
send   write

6 **Work in pairs. Talk about the best day of your life.**

What was the best day of your life? What happened?

BOB GELDOF

Bob Geldof was born in Dublin on 5 October 1954. In 1975 he started a ro[ck] band called the 'Boomtown Rats' and he became a famous pop star. But no[w] he is best-known as the man who made millions of pounds to help the peop[le] of Africa.

It all began in October 1984, when Geldof saw the television news about Ethiopia: millions of people were dying of hunger. He was very upset, so he decided to make and sell a record, and to give the money to Ethiopia. He an[d] Midge Ure wrote a song called *Do They Know It's Christmas?* and Geldof aske[d] some pop star friends to record the song. He called the group 'Band Aid' an[d] Sunday 25 November 1984, they recorded the song in London. Two weeks later the record was in the shops. It sold millions of copies and made £8 milli[on] In December 1984, Geldof went to Ethiopia and saw the starving people an[d] the civil war. He was very shocked.

In March 1985, Geldof started to plan the Live Aid concert in London. But h[e] also wanted a concert at the same time in America. He chose Philadelphia. H[e] worked very hard for weeks to organise the concerts. Finally, on 13 July at 1[2] noon, the concert in London started. At 5pm the concert in Philadelphia star[ted] and Live Aid continued, with one band from America, then one band from Britain, until 10pm. Then the London concert finished and the Philadelphia concert continued for another five hours. Every hour, Bob Geldof came on [TV] and asked for money. In all, Live Aid made £50 million. When the concert wa[s] over he said, 'I think this is the best day of my life'.

Live Aid sent food, medicine, clothing, blankets and toys to Ethiopia. But the war and the famine continued. What's happening there today? Can you do anything to help?

AND LIVE AID

7 Work in pairs.

STUDENT A   Turn to page 110 for your instructions.
STUDENT B   Turn to page 112 for your instructions.

8 Write three questions beginning *Where ...?*

Where was Bob Geldof born ?

Now work in pairs and answer your partner's questions.

9 🔲 Here is some more information about Bob Geldof. But some of it is wrong. Listen and circle the wrong information.

Bob Geldof toured the world with his successful jazz band, the Boomtown Rats. One of their most popular songs was 'I don't like Tuesdays'. He also acted in four films. In 1982, he played an Irish boy in the film *The Wall* with Pink Floyd. In 1986, he acted with Mel Smith in a film called *Number Three*. He went back to Africa that year, and travelled through eight countries from Mali to Ethiopia. In 1986, he organised Sport Aid and made another 30 million pounds, and he became 'Sir' Bob Geldof because of his work for Africa. He wrote a play about his life called *Is That It?*, which was published in 1986. The same year, he married Paula Yates, whom he met in 1979. They have two sons.

Listen again and correct the information.

10 Work in pairs. Check your answers to activity 9 with your partner. Read the new version aloud and stress the information you have corrected.

Bob Geldof toured the world with his successful <u>rock</u> band, the Boomtown Rats.

11 Write sentences.

The Boomtown Rats weren't a jazz band. They were a rock band.

Bob Geldof didn't act in four films. He acted in two films.

12 Write six sentences about the most important events in Bob Geldof's life. Compare your sentences with other students.

13 Work in pairs. Describe three of the most important events in your life. Say what happened, and why it was important.

Now write a short paragraph about one important event.

14 Find out the past simple of these irregular verbs.

run   sit   swim   cost   wear
sing   speak   understand
bring   say   find   know   hear

What's the past tense of 'run'?

In this lesson you practise:
• **Talking about the past (2)**
• **Regular and irregular verbs**
Now turn to page 72 and look at the STRUCTURES TO LEARN and the WORDS TO REMEMBER.

1 Kate and Nick are going on a safari holiday in East Africa. They are staying in hotels. Ask and say which of these items they should take.

They should take . . . because . . .
They (don't) need to take . . .

2 ▭ Listen and tick the items Kate and Nick are taking on holiday. Check your answers to activity 1.

Now ask and say which items they are taking.

3 Ask and say.

When are you going on holiday?
Where are you going?
Where's that?
What's it like?

What's the weather like?
Where are you staying?
What do you need to take?

4 Read the postcard. Decide where these words could go.

yesterday   small   boat   very   today

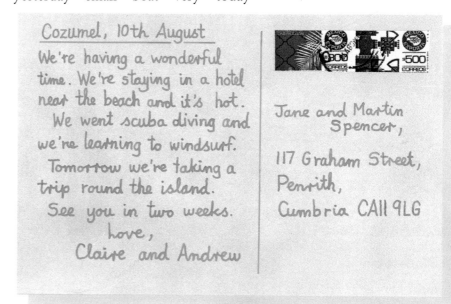

Cozumel, 10th August
We're having a wonderful time. We're staying in a hotel near the beach and it's hot. We went scuba diving and we're learning to windsurf. Tomorrow we're taking a trip round the island. See you in two weeks.
love,
Claire and Andrew

Jane and Martin Spencer,
117 Graham Street,
Penrith,
Cumbria CA11 9LG

5 Write a holiday postcard to a friend. Say:

– where you are staying
– what the weather is like
– what you did yesterday
– what you are doing today/tomorrow

6 You can survive as a traveller if you can:

– give personal details
– understand a menu
– order something to eat and drink
– ask how much things cost
– ask for directions
– talk about the weather
– ask for help when you don't understand

Can you do all these things in English?

7 Look at the cover of the book. What do you think it is about?

Now read the passage quickly and check.

A pioneer of the 20th century

Beryl Markham . . . born in England in 1902. In 1906, her father. . . to live in Africa, and . . . her with him. He . . . on a farm and Beryl . . . him to train racehorses. But in 1919, it didn't rain for months, and they . . . the farm. Her father . . . Africa for Peru, but Beryl . . . in Kenya. At the age of eighteen, she . . . a racehorse trainer's licence, the first woman in Africa to do so. In 1927, she . . . Mansfield Markham, the first of three marriages, and in 1929 they . . . a son.

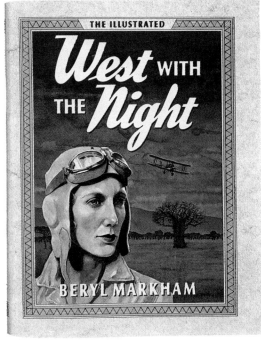

THE ILLUSTRATED
West WITH
THE *Night*

BERYL MARKHAM

   In 1931, Beryl Markham . . . flying, carrying letters, passengers and supplies all over East Africa in her small plane. In September 1936, she . . . the first person to fly solo across the Atlantic from east to west – she . . . in England and . . . to Nova Scotia where she . . . twenty-one hours and five minutes later. Beryl Markham . . . a famous book called *West with the Night*, published in 1942. She . . . in Kenya in 1986.

8 Complete the passage with the past tense forms of these verbs.

be   become   die   fly   get   go   have   help   land   leave   marry
sell   start   stay   take   take off   work   write

9 Write sentences correcting these statements about Beryl Markham's life.

*1 She didn't go to West Africa in 1906.
   She went to East Africa.*

1 Beryl Markham went to West Africa in 1906.
2 Her mother took her to Africa.
3 She married Mansfield Markham in 1928.
4 Mansfield Markham was her second husband.
5 They had a daughter in 1929.
6 Beryl started flying in 1930.
7 She flew across the Atlantic from west to east.
8 She wrote a book called *West with the Light*.

Now underline the two words that are different in each of your answers. Then read the sentences aloud and stress the underlined words.

10 Write five sentences about important events in your life. Think about these questions.

When and where were you born?
Where did you live as a child?
Where did you go to your first school and what did/didn't you like?
When did you meet someone important to you?
When did you start work?

Now work in pairs. Ask your partner questions about his/her life. As you listen, take notes.

Then write a short paragraph about your partner's life.

11 Read these letters.

ANY QUESTIONS?

WRITE TO THE LANGUAGE DOCTOR

QUESTION   I'm not sure how to write the date in English. For example, do you write 10 July or 10th July? Do you write July 10th or July 10? Can you write 10.7.89? And how do you say it?
Carlos, Guadalajara

ANSWER   You can write the date in all the ways you suggest. You can write 10.7.89 to mean 10th July – but be careful! In Britain, 7.10.89 means 7th October. If someone asks the date, we say, 'It's the tenth of July' or 'It's July the tenth'. But when we talk about events, we use a preposition:

   on + day/date
I met her *on* Monday, July 10th.

   in + month/year
I'm going to Spain *in* July.
I started work *in* 1989.

Have you got any questions about English? Write a letter to the language doctor and give it to your teacher.

STRUCTURES TO LEARN

Describing places

Where's Timbuktoo?	It's in the middle/ centre of Mali.
What's the capital of China?	Beijing.
What's the population of Bangkok?	About five and a half million.
What's Reykjavik like?	It's (very/quite) interesting.

Prepositions of place: *in, on*

Naples is *in* Italy. It's *on* the coast.
London is *in* the south of England. It's *on* the River Thames.
Innsbruck is *in* the mountains.

For more prepositions of place, see *Lessons 2, 13* and *14 LANGUAGE STUDY*.

WORDS TO REMEMBER

capital /kæpɪtəl/   centre /sɛntə/   city /sɪti/
coast /kəʊst/   middle /mɪdəl/
mountain /maʊntɪn/   population /pɒpjəleɪʃən/
port /pɔːt/   river /rɪvə/
tourist centre /tʊərɪst sɛntə/   village /vɪlɪdʒ/

east /iːst/   north /nɔːθ/   north-east /nɔːθiːst/
north-west /nɔːθwɛst/   south /saʊθ/
south-east /saʊθiːst/   south-west /saʊθwɛst/
west /wɛst/

quite /kwaɪt/   very /vɛri/

big /bɪg/   busy /bɪzi/   commercial /kəmɜːʃəl/
crowded /kraʊdɪd/   dangerous /deɪndʒərəs/
industrial /ɪndʌstrɪəl/   interesting /ɪntrəstɪŋ/
modern /mɒdən/   noisy /nɔɪzi/   old /əʊld/
pretty /prɪti/   quiet /kwaɪət/   small /smɔːl/

thousand /θaʊzənd/   million /mɪljən/

PRACTICE EXERCISES

❶ Underline the stressed syllables.

Paris	Granada	Calcutta
Caracas	Vienna	Birmingham
Madrid	Athens	Oslo
London	Milan	Helsinki

Which words have the stress pattern ●•?
Which words have the stress pattern •●•?

▣ **Listen and check. Repeat the words.**

❷ Underline the most important words.

1 Nottingham is a commercial and industrial town in the middle of England.
2 Santiago de Compostela is a beautiful town in the north of Spain.
3 Athens is the capital of Greece. It's in the south.
4 Calcutta is a large commercial city in the east of India.
5 Mombasa is a large port on the east coast of Africa.
6 Recife is a busy commercial city in the north-east of Brazil.

▣ **Now listen and check. The stressed words are the most important words.**

❸ ▣ Answer the questions.

Example: *What's Naples like?*
It's a big city in the south of Italy.

1 Naples: big city/south of Italy
2 Rio: busy city/coast of Brazil
3 Glasgow: industrial city/west of Scotland
4 Nice: beautiful tourist centre/south of France
5 Montevideo: large port/River Plate
6 Toledo: pretty town/centre of Spain

❹ Complete the paragraph.

Montpellier is . . . old city . . . the south . . . France. It's got . . . population . . . about four hundred thousand people. It's . . . tourist centre and . . . important commercial city. It's very interesting . . . very pretty.

▣ **Listen and check.**

STRUCTURES TO LEARN

Talking about the future (1): Arrangements
You can use the present continuous when you talk about future arrangements.
  What are you doing next week?
  We're flying to Oslo.

For information about how to form the present continuous, see *Lesson 14 LANGUAGE STUDY.*

Question words
  Which countries are they visiting?
  When is your birthday?
  Where are they going in April?
  What's the date today?
  How many performances are they doing?

Asking and saying the date
  What's the date today?
  It's the seventh of November.

  When's her birthday?
  It's (on) April the sixteenth.

Prepositions of time: *on, in*
You use *in* for months:
  I'm going there *in* April.
You use *on* for dates:
  I'm going there *on* April the sixteenth.

For more prepositions of time, see *Lessons 10, 13* and *19 LANGUAGE STUDY.*

WORDS TO REMEMBER

(happy) birthday /(hæpi) bɜːθdeɪ/   date /deɪt/
fly (v) /flaɪ/   home /həʊm/
performance /pəfɔːməns/   yesterday /jɛstədeɪ/

first /fɜːst/   then /ðɛn/   after that /ɑːftə ðæt/
finally /faɪnəli/

January /dʒænjʊəri/   February /Fɛbrʊəri/
March /mɑːtʃ/   April /eɪprəl/   May /meɪ/
June /dʒuːn/   July /dʒuːlaɪ/   August /ɔːgəst/
September /sɛptɛmbə/   October /ɒktəʊbə/
November /nəʊvɛmbə/   December /dɪsɛmbə/

1st first /fɜːst/   2nd second /sɛkənd/
3rd third /θɜːd/   4th fourth /fɔːθ/
5th fifth /fɪfθ/   6th sixth /sɪksθ/
7th seventh /sɛvənθ/   8th eighth /eɪtθ/
9th ninth /naɪnθ/   10th tenth /tɛnθ/
11th eleventh /ilɛvənθ/   12th twelfth /twɛlfθ/

PRACTICE EXERCISES

❶ ▪▪ Listen and repeat. Make sure your voice rises and falls with the arrows.

1 – What are you doing next Saturday?

  – We're visiting some friends.

2 – Which countries are they visiting?

  – They're going to China, Korea and Japan.

3 – When's your birthday?

  – It's on the twentieth of June.

Now read the sentences aloud.

❷ ▪▪ Ask questions. Listen to Sally and match the dates with the events.

Example: *2nd March*
        What are you doing on the second of March?
        I'm going on holiday.

1	2nd March	visit friends
2	4th April	go to a concert
3	12th May	drive to Manchester
4	23rd July	go on holiday
5	30 August	get married
6	1st September	fly to Paris

❸ ▪▪ Answer questions about the events in exercise 2.

Example: *What's Sally doing on the second of March?*
        She's going on holiday.

❹ ▪▪ Ask questions. Listen to the answers and write the dates.

Example: *Tony is leaving school.*
        When is he leaving school?
        On the thirteenth of July.

1 Tony/leave school   13.7
2 Mr and Mrs Porter/go to Milan
3 Katya/play at a concert
4 Boris and Tanya/get married
5 James/start a new job

❺ Now write sentences.

Example: 1 Tony is leaving school on
        13 th July.

STRUCTURES TO LEARN

Talking about the weather
What's the weather like in your country?
It rains in winter.
It sometimes snows in winter.
It's hot in summer.
It's usually quite cold in winter.

Adverbs of frequency
You can use these to say how often things happen.
always (100% – all the time)
usually (90% – nearly all the time)
often (66% – much of the time)
sometimes (33% – some of the time)
never (0% – none of the time)

In Siberia it's *always* cold in winter.
In São Paulo it's *usually* hot in summer.
In London it *often* rains.
In Paris it *sometimes* snows.
It *never* snows in the Sahara.

For some adverbial phrases of frequency, see *Lesson 13 LANGUAGE STUDY*.

Giving reasons (2)
You can use *because* and *so* to give reasons.
We should take umbrellas *because* it rains a lot.
It rains a lot *so* we should take umbrellas.

Saying what is necessary / advisable
We (don't) need to take a sleeping bag.
We should take sunglasses.

WORDS TO REMEMBER

often /ɒfən/   sometimes /sʌmtaɪmz/
usually /juːʒʊəli/

cold /kəʊld/   cool /kuːl/   dry /draɪ/   hot /hɒt/
rain (v) /reɪn/   snow (v) /snəʊ/   summer /sʌmə/
warm /wɔːm/   weather /weðə/   wet /wet/
winter /wɪntə/

bring /brɪŋ/   take /teɪk/

alarm clock /əlɑːm klɒk/   anorak /ænəræk/
camera /kæmrə/   corkscrew /kɔːkskruː/
first aid kit /fɜːst eɪd kɪt/   gloves /glʌvz/
key /kiː/   knife /naɪf/   photo /fəʊtəʊ/
photograph /fəʊtəgrɑːf/
razor /reɪzə/   rucksack /rʌksæk/   scarf /skɑːf/
(pair of) shorts (/peər əv) ʃɔːts/
sleeping bag /sliːpɪŋ bæg/   socks /sɒks/
sunglasses /sʌnglɑːsɪz/
swimming costume /swɪmɪŋ kɒstjuːm/
torch /tɔːtʃ/   traveller's cheques /trævələz tʃeks/
whistle /wɪsəl/

PRACTICE EXERCISES

❶ **Say these words.**

/kuːl/ /wet/ /hɒt/ /snəʊ/ /wɪntə/ /reɪn/

▪️ **Listen and check. Repeat the words.**

❷ **Complete the dialogue.**

A What's the . . . like in Vienna?
B It's usually quite . . . in summer and it's very cold in . . . .
A Does it ever snow?
B It often . . . in winter, and it stays . . . until April.
A Does it often . . . ?
B Yes, it rains in March and April.

▪️ **Listen and check.**

❸ **Put the adverbs in the correct position.**

1 In Amsterdam it rains in winter. (often)
2 It snows in the mountains in winter. (always)
3 It's hot in London in summer. (sometimes)
4 It's warm in Manchester in summer. (never)
5 In Reykjavik it's cold in winter. (usually)

▪️ **Listen and check.**

❹ **Match the advice with the reasons.**

You should . . .	because . . .
1 wear a hat	the evenings are cool.
2 eat in restaurants	March and April are quite wet.
3 take lots of money	the sea is very warm.
4 take a pullover	things are very expensive.
5 take an umbrella in spring	the sun's very hot.
6 take a swimming costume	the food isn't very good in hotels.

▪️ **Listen and check.**

❺ ▪️ **Answer the questions with the reasons in exercise 4.**

Example: *Why should I wear a hat?*
Because the sun's very hot.

❻ **Write sentences giving advice. Connect the phrases in exercise 4 with *so*.**

Example: 1 *The sun's very hot so...*

▪️ **Listen and check.**

STRUCTURES TO LEARN

Talking about the past (1)
The past tense form is the same for all persons **except** in the verb *be*.

Past tense: *be*

Affirmative   **Negative**

I was	Full form	Short form
you were	I was not	I wasn't
he/she/it was	you were not	you weren't
	he/she/it was not	he/she/it wasn't
we were	we were not	we weren't
they were	they were not	they weren't

Questions   **Short answers**

Was I/he/she/it?	Yes, I/he/she/it was.
	No, I/he/she/it wasn't.
	Yes, you/we/they were.
Were you/we/they?	No, you/we/ they weren't.

Past simple tense

Affirmative

I/you/he/she/it/we/they started

Negative

Full form	Short form
I/you/he/she/it/ we/they did not start	I/you/he/she/it/ we/they didn't start

Questions   **Short answers**

Did I/you/he/she/it/ we/they start?	Yes, I/you/he/she/it/ we/they did.
	No, I/you/he/she/it/ we/they didn't.

Expressions of past time
yesterday   last week   last month   last year

ago means *before now.*
Today's Monday. We went to the cinema two days *ago* – on Saturday.

For more information about the past simple tense, see *Lesson 20 LANGUAGE STUDY.*

Prepositions of time: *in, at, on*
in March   *in* 1987   *in* the morning
on Saturday   *at* the weekend

For more prepositions of time, see *Lessons 10, 13* and *17 LANGUAGE STUDY.*

WORDS TO REMEMBER

between /bɪtwiːn/   boring /bɔːrɪŋ/
century /sɛntʃəri/   comfortable /kʌmftəbəl/
early /ɜːli/   flight /flaɪt/   hour /auə/
journey /dʒɜːni/   land (v) /lænd/   later /leɪtə/
long /lɒŋ/   passenger /pæsɪndʒə/   plane /pleɪn/
remember /rɪmɛmbə/   route /ruːt/   sure /ʃuə/
tiring /taɪərɪŋ/   travel /trævəl/

PRACTICE EXERCISES

❶ Write these words in the correct column.

/d/   /t/   /ɪd/

finished   happened   landed   liked   started
stayed   stopped   travelled   visited

▭▭ **Listen and check. Repeat the words.**

❷ Complete the sentences with *did, didn't, was, wasn't, were* or *weren't.*

1 – . . . you have a good flight?
– Yes, I . . . .
2 – Were there many passengers?
– No, there . . . .
3 – . . . you have anything to eat?
– No, I . . . hungry.
4 – . . . you get up early?
– Yes, it . . . an early flight.
5 – . . . it a long journey?
– No, it . . . . It . . . take very long at all.
6 – . . . the plane stop anywhere?
– No, it . . . .

▭▭ **Listen and check.**

❸ ▭▭ Answer questions.

Example: *Did Jack go to Venice last year?*
No, he didn't.

1 Did Jack go to Venice last year?   ✗
2 Did he go to Florence?   ✓
3 Did he stay in a hotel?   ✓
4 Did he stay with friends?   ✗
5 Were there lots of people?   ✗
6 Was the journey tiring?   ✓
7 Did he go to many restaurants?   ✗
8 Did he enjoy his stay?   ✓

❹ Write sentences about Jack's holiday.

Example: 1 *He didn't go to Venice.*

▭▭ **Listen and check.**

STRUCTURES TO LEARN

Talking about the past (2)

Past simple tense

You form the past simple tense of most regular verbs by adding *-ed*.

ask	call	start
asked	called	started

You form the past simple tense of verbs which end in *-e* by adding *-d*.

dance	decide	continue
danced	decided	continued

You pronounce *-ed* in three ways.

/t/	/d/	/ɪd/
asked	called	started
danced	continued	decided

Here is the past simple form of some other regular verbs.

carry	play	stop
carried	played	stopped

Past simple tense: irregular verbs

Here are some irregular verbs.

Infinitive	Past simple
become	became
begin	began
choose	chose
come	came
go	went
make	made
see	saw
sell	sold
send	sent
write	wrote

For a list of all the irregular verbs which appear in this book, turn to page 109. For more information about the past tense, see *Lesson 19 LANGUAGE STUDY*.

Contrastive stress

When you disagree with a statement and want to contradict it, you correct the wrong information and stress it.

The Boomtown Rats were a jazz band.
They weren't a <u>jazz</u> band – they were a <u>rock</u> band.

WORDS TO REMEMBER

band /bænd/   best /bɛst/   famous /feɪməs/
news /njuːz/   pop star /pɒp stɑː/
record (n) /rɛkɔːd/   song /sɒŋ/

act /ækt/   be born /biː bɔːn/   become /bikʌm/
begin /bɪgɪn/   call /kɔːl/   choose /tʃuːz/
come /kʌm/   continue /kəntɪnjuː/
decide /disaɪd/   give /gɪv/   happen /hæpən/
make /meɪk/   marry /mæri/   plan /plæn/
record (v) /rɪkɔːd/   see /siː/   sell /sɛl/
send /sɛnd/   talk /tɔːk/

PRACTICE EXERCISES

❶ Write *in*, *at*, *on* or *–*.

1 I was born . . . 20th June, 1954.
2 He started school . . . 1960.
3 I went to visit my parents . . . the weekend.
4 We saw the latest Coppola film . . . a week ago.
5 She began her English course . . . October.
6 I stopped work . . . five o'clock . . . the afternoon.

📼 Listen and check.

❷ Listen and underline the most important word in each of the responses.

Example: *Bob Geldof was born in Liverpool in 1954.*

1 No, he was born in <u>Dublin</u> in 1954.
2 No, he started a rock band in 1975.
3 No, Band Aid recorded a song for Ethiopia.
4 No, the concert was in July 1985.
5 No, Live Aid made £50 million.

📼 Now listen again and correct the statements.

❸ 📼 Ask questions about Bob Geldof.

Example: *He went to Ethiopia.*
        When did he go to Ethiopia?

1 when/go to Ethiopia
2 where/record the Band Aid song
3 what/send to Ethiopia
4 when/organise the Live Aid concert
5 what/say after the concert

❹ Write answers to the questions in exercise 3.

Example: *1 He went to Ethiopia in October 1984.*

1 in October 1984	4 in 1985
2 in London	5 'This is the best
3 money	day of my life.'

📼 Listen and check.

Body and Mind 5

How healthy are you... in body and in mind?
How people live: Eating habits round the world
Family connections - famous parents with famous sons and daughters
Britain in view: the education system
Spotlight on special people - the youngest, the oldest and the greatest
PLUS
Meet the next Einstein: a ten year-old American boy

Can you say

NO?

A Let's go to the cinema tonight.

B How about a game of football?

C Would you like to go to a rock concert this evening?

What do you say when you don't want to do something? You can't just say no, you have to make an excuse. Why don't you say you don't feel well?

Here are some excuses:

I'm sorry but . . .
> I've got a headache.
> I've got backache.
> my leg hurts.
> my hand hurts.
> I feel tired.
> I feel sick.
> I don't feel well.

❶ **Look at the pictures in CAN YOU SAY NO? and make excuses.**

📼 **Listen and check.**

❷ **Make excuses which begin *I've got . . .*, *My . . . hurt(s)*, or *I feel . . .* . Use these words.**

a cold   arm   faint   shoulder   toothache   a stiff neck   a sore throat
hot   foot   a runny nose   a cough   stomachache   a temperature

❸ **Work in pairs.**

STUDENT A   **Invite Student B to do something. If he/she refuses, make other suggestions.**
STUDENT B   **Refuse Student A's invitations. Make good excuses!**

❹ 📼 **Listen and repeat.**

MAN   I don't feel well.
WOMAN   What's the matter?
MAN   I've got a headache, and a temperature.
WOMAN   Oh, I am sorry. Perhaps you've got flu.

❺ **Find out what these illnesses are.**

flu   a hangover   food poisoning   sunstroke

Find the words for two more illnesses.

❻ **Work in pairs.**

STUDENT A   **Choose an illness and say what's the matter with you.**
STUDENT B   **Listen to your partner and try to guess what the illness is.**

Healthy body

Being healthy is not just a question of physical fitness. It's also a question of your self-confidence and your intellectual, organisational and artistic abilities.

So how healthy are you . . . in body and in mind?

1 ....
These days we know more about our bodies, and we take more care of them. So do you eat sensibly? And do you take exercise every day? How do you feel when you run up the stairs quickly? Or when you swim 500 metres?

2 ....
We admire people who play a musical instrument well, so what about you? Do you play the piano or the guitar? Perhaps you paint or draw beautifully. And what about poetry or dance or . . .? Well, what can you do?

7 Read HEALTHY BODY, HEALTHY MIND and give each paragraph a title. Choose from the list below.

How artistic are you?
How confident are you?
How fit are you?
How organised are you?
How intellectual are you?

Healthy mind

3 ....
We know it's important to be careful and efficient at work or at school. But what about at home? If four people come for dinner, what about cooking a meal for them? In less than an hour? And can you find your dentist's address easily? Or your doctor's phone number?

4 ....
Many people speak at least two languages fluently. You certainly know one, and now you're learning English. But what about a third language? And a fourth? And in these days of calculators, what about adding and subtracting numbers accurately in your head?

5 ....
Standing up and speaking to a large group of people is not easy. Can you do it? And what happens if you get bad service in a restaurant? Do you find it easy to complain?

8 Find the adverbs in the passage which match these adjectives.

quick   fluent   accurate   easy   beautiful   sensible   good

Write them down and look at the spelling. Which one is irregular?

Now write the adverbs formed from these adjectives.

happy   confident   careful   quiet   noisy   comfortable   safe

9 Read this sentence from the passage.

How do you feel when you run up the stairs quickly?

Now put a different adverb in each of these sentences. Choose from the adverbs in activity 8.

1 Can you speak two or more languages?
2 Can you speak to a large group of people?
3 Can you find your doctor's phone number?
4 Can you add and subtract numbers in your head?

10 Write a questionnaire to find out:

How healthy are you . . . in body and in mind?

Write questions which begin with *Can you . . . ?* Use the passage to help you.

Now write three more questions of your own for the questionnaire.

11 Ask and answer questions about what you can do. Say if you can do things well.

A Can you speak three languages fluently?
B Yes, I can./No, I can't.
  I can speak French (quite) well.
  I can't speak Italian very well at all.

12 Work in groups. Find three things you can all do.

A I can swim half a kilometre.
B So can I!/Can you? I can't.

13 What can you do if you don't understand a word when you are reading?

– You can decide what part of speech the word is – noun, verb, adverb, etc.
– You can look for clues in the context.
– You can ask another student or your teacher.
– Then you can check in the dictionary.

Now read something in English and use these techniques.

In this lesson you practise:
● **Making invitations (2)**
● **Asking and saying how you feel**
● **Talking about ability**
● **Adjectives and adverbs**
Now turn to page 86 and look at the STRUCTURES TO LEARN and the WORDS TO REMEMBER.

1 Ask and say what you eat in your country, and when.

eggs toast bacon cakes cheese bread potatoes steak
curry soup sausage fruit rice fish yoghurt cereal

A What do you eat for breakfast/lunch/dinner?
B In Greece we eat cakes for breakfast.

2 Read EATING IN BRITAIN and give each paragraph a title. Choose from this list.

Table manners   Meal times
Fast food   Quality and cost
Typical food

Be careful: there is one extra title.

3 Find this sentence in EATING IN BRITAIN. It doesn't belong.

Most children like hamburgers.

Read the paragraphs again and find two more sentences which don't belong.

4 Read these statements. Decide whether they are true or false for Britain. Correct the false statements.

1 Most people have a small breakfast.
2 Lunch is usually at two o'clock.
3 Lunch is a light meal.
4 Dinner is a big meal.
5 Dinner takes about an hour.
6 Home cooking is very bad.
7 Most people are too fat.
8 It's easy to buy the food you want.
9 Food for two people costs about £30 a week.
10 A restaurant meal costs about £10 a person.

Eating in Britain

1

In Britain we have three meals a day: breakfast when we get up in the morning, lunch at about one o'clock and dinner between six and eight o'clock in the evening.

2

Some people have eggs and bacon for breakfast, but most people only have cereal or fruit juice, and toast and marmalade with tea or coffee. Supermarkets open early in the morning. Lunch is usually a light meal of salad or a sandwich. Dinner is the main meal and it takes about half an hour. There is usually meat and vegetables, and then a dessert.

3

When you don't want any more to eat, put your knife and fork together in the centre of your plate. Most children like hamburgers. You shouldn't smoke during the meal.

4

Eating habits in Britain are changing. People are eating better because they want to stay slim and healthy. Home cooking is quite good and it is easy to buy the food you want. Two people can eat quite well for £30 a week. Cigarettes cost over £1.50 a packet. But restaurant meals are very expensive, costing £15 to £20 a person.

5 You are going to hear people talking about eating habits in Holland, India and Canada. First, read the notes in the chart in HOW PEOPLE LIVE. Look up any words you do not understand.

▭▭ Now listen and fill in the chart with the letters H (Holland) and I (India).

6 Talk about eating habits in Canada. Use the other notes in the chart.

▭▭ Now listen and check.

7 Work in pairs. Use the headings in the chart to talk about eating habits in your country.

Now write a paragraph about eating habits in your country. Use EATING IN BRITAIN to help you.

8 ▭▭ Listen and read.

A In Britain most people have a small breakfast.
B Do you have a larger breakfast in your country?
A And lunch is a light meal. Many people only have a sandwich.
B Is lunch a heavier meal in your country?

9 ▭▭ Listen and repeat.

small	smaller
large	larger
light	lighter
heavy	heavier

HOW PEOPLE LIVE

EATING HABITS

Typical breakfast	Rice or curry, fried fish, tea	[I]	Bread, butter, cheese, jam, milk or tea	[H]	Toast, jam, coffee, sometimes pancakes [ ]
Time of the main meal	5pm to 6pm [ ]		6pm	[ ]	9.30pm to 10.30pm [ ]
Typical food at the main meal	Potatoes, vegetables, meat, pudding or yoghurt	[ ]	Bread, green vegetables, pulses, a sweet, betel leaf	[ ]	meat, potatoes, salad, fruit pie, ice cream [ ]
Length of the meal	More than an hour	[ ]	15 minutes to half an hour	[ ]	Three quarters or half an hour [ ]
Table manners	Never put your hands under the table	[ ]	Cut food first, put knife down while you eat, one hand under the table	[ ]	Eat with fingers of right hand, serve yourself with left hand [ ]

Are eating habits in your country the same as in Britain? Or are they different?
Is breakfast in your country smaller or larger than in Britain?
Is lunch earlier or later?
Is lunch lighter or heavier?
Is dinner bigger or smaller?
Do you think home cooking is better or worse?
Do you think most people are fatter or slimmer?
Is it easier to buy the food you want or more difficult?
Is food cheaper or more expensive?
Are restaurants more expensive or cheaper?

⑩ Work in pairs and answer the questions in HOW PEOPLE LIVE. Use the true statements in activity 4 to help you.

If the answers are the same, make sentences like this:
We have a small breakfast *too.*
If the answers are different, make sentences like this:
Lunch is *heavier* in Italy *than* in Britain.

⑪ Look at the spelling of the comparative adjectives below.

small → smaller
large → larger
fat → fatter
heavy → heavier
difficult → more difficult
good → better

Now write the comparative form of these adjectives.

big   early   expensive   cheap
bad   late   easy   light   slim

⑫ Write six sentences using comparative adjectives.
Apples are larger than grapes.
English is easier than Chinese.

Now work in pairs. Write your partner's sentences another way.
Grapes are smaller than apples.
Chinese is more difficult than English.

⑬ What do you eat and drink? Look at the words in this lesson, and in Lessons 7 and 9, and write them under these headings: *breakfast, lunch, dinner, never.*

In this lesson you practise:
● **Making comparisons (1): Comparative adjectives**
Now turn to page 87 and look at the STRUCTURES TO LEARN and the WORDS TO REMEMBER.

family connections

❶ 📼 **Listen and read.**

KATE   This is my brother, Robert.

PETER   He looks like you.

KATE   Yes, we've got the same mouth.

PETER   And does your sister look like you too?

KATE   No, she's got long dark hair.

PETER   And how old is she?

KATE   She's younger than me. She's sixteen.

❷ 📼 **Listen and repeat.**

He looks like you.
We've got the same mouth.
She's got long dark hair.
How old is she?
She's younger than me.
She's sixteen.

Now match the sentences with these stress patterns.

●●∙∙   ●●∙●

∙∙∙●●   ●●∙∙●

●∙●●   ∙∙●●●

Debbie Reynolds

Jamie Lee Curtis

A

B

❸ Write the stress patterns for these sentences.

You look like her.
She's got the same nose.
He's got short fair hair.
How tall is he?
I'm shorter than him.
He's nineteen.

📼 **Listen and check.**

Now make more sentences with the same stress patterns.

❹ Ask and say.

A   Does your daughter look like you?

B   Yes, she does. She's got the same nose. And she's got blue eyes too.

A   Do you look like your father?

B   No, I don't. I'm slimmer than him, and he's got fair hair and big ears.

❺ Ask and say how old you are and how tall you are.

A   How old are you?
B   I'm eighteen.

A   How tall are you?
B   I'm one metre seventy-five.

Find out the average age and height of the people in your class.

These people are all actors and actresses – and their talent runs in the family. They are famous parents, and famous sons and daughters. Can you find the family connections?

Michael Douglas

6 Work in pairs. Look at the photos in FAMILY CONNECTIONS and match the relatives.

A I think this is Michael Douglas's father. He looks like him.
B Yes, he's got the same mouth.
A And that's Debbie's daughter.
B I'm not sure. She's isn't tall enough. And her hair's too dark.

7 🔲 Listen to three descriptions and point at the people.

8 Read this description of one of the people in FAMILY CONNECTIONS. Who is it?

He's slim and quite tall. He's at least forty, but he looks younger. He's got fairly short brown hair, and he's wearing a striped shirt, a suit and a tie. He's very handsome, and he looks like his father.

Now turn to page 114 for your instructions.

9 Write a description of one of the people in the photos. Use the description in activity 8 to help you.

Now work in pairs. Show your description to your partner. Read your partner's description and guess who he/she is describing.

He's She's	(not) very fairly quite	thin. slim. fat. tall. short.

He's She's	got	long short straight curly	brown dark fair blonde red grey	hair.

He's She's	wearing . . .

10 Work in groups of three.

STUDENT A   Turn to page 111 for your instructions.
STUDENT B   Turn to page 113 for your instructions.
STUDENT C   Turn to page 114 for your instructions.

11 Write the names and roles of two more characters in your film on two pieces of paper. Give them to the other directors in your group.

Now write a letter to the other directors. Suggest suitable people in your class to play the characters and describe what they look like.

I think Pierre is the best person to play Luke Spacerider's assistant in your film, because . . .

12 Write down five words from this lesson. Think of words which rhyme with them. Then tell another student the rhyming words. He/She must think of the words you wrote.

In this lesson you practise:
● Asking for and giving personal details (5)
● Describing appearance
● Making comparisons (2)
● Personal pronouns: Subject and Object
● Question words: *who, what*
Now turn to page 88 and look at the STRUCTURES TO LEARN and the WORDS TO REMEMBER.

❶ **This lesson is about education and includes these words. Which of them do you already know?**

homework sport Latin teacher art English maths lesson physics uniform chemistry holidays geography rule history subject pupil school exam(ination) university

Now find eight words for school subjects.

❷ ▭ **Listen and check the subjects. Repeat the words.**

Now find words with the same stress patterns.

● •   ● • •

 teacher   chemistry

❸ **Talk about your favourite subjects.**

A What was your favourite subject?
B History.
C My favourite subjects are music and art.

❹ **Match the BRITAIN IN VIEW photos and the captions. There are two extra captions.**

❺ **Work in pairs. Answer questions 1–4 in the chart for Britain.**

	Britain	Your country
1 When do pupils start school?		
2 When can pupils leave school?		
3 How many subjects do they study?		
4 How many hours a day are they at school?		
5 When do pupils take the first public exam?		
6 How many pupils go to university? (%)		
7 How many pupils go to private schools? (%)		
8 When do pupils take the second public exam?		
9 How many pupils leave school at sixteen? (%)		
10 How many weeks holiday do they get in a year?		

❻ **Work in pairs.**

STUDENT A   Turn to page 111 for your instructions.
STUDENT B   Turn to page 113 for your instructions.

❼ **Work together. Complete the column for Britain.**

A When do pupils take the second public exam?
B How many pupils go to university?

Now complete the column for your country.

❽ **Compare the education system in Britain with your country.**

In Britain they start school   It's the same as France.
earlier than in my country.   It's different from Mexico.

❾ **Write sentences describing the education system in your country.**

Britain in view

the EDUCATION system

- Children start school at 5 years old.
- Children can leave at 16 but 25% stay on until they are 18.
- They study about ten subjects, including art and woodwork.
- The day begins at 9am and ends at 3.30pm.
- Nearly every child does some kind of sport.
- People go to university when they are 18 or 19.

Is the system the same in your country?

10 Read and say what the people in the photos are talking about. Choose from the list below.

foreign language lessons
exams   sport   homework
school rules

Now find three words which you don't understand but your partner does.

11 Say what the people think about school life.

... thinks there's too *much* ...
... thinks there *are* too *many* ...
... does*n't* think there's/there are enough ...

12 ▣▣ Listen and read. Decide whether B agrees or disagrees with A.

1 A I don't think we should learn Latin now.
   B Nor do I.
2 A There are too many foreign language lessons.
   B Yes, but languages are very useful.
3 A I don't think that there's enough sport.
   B I agree.
4 A I think there's too much homework.
   B So do I.
5 A I think that there are too many exams.
   B Well, I'm not sure.
6 A There aren't enough school rules.
   B I don't agree.

13 Work in pairs. Say what you think about the following.

foreign language lessons
exams   sport   homework
school rules   Latin
school holidays
school leaving age   uniform
size of classes   universities

Find out what other students in your class think.

'When I was at school, I wasn't very good at academic subjects, but I spent a lot of time playing football for the school team, and tennis. It gives pupils who aren't so intelligent the opportunity to do something really well, and I think there should be more of it ...'

David

'Of course, when I actually went to England and Spain for the first time, I could talk a lot about Shakespeare and Cervantes, but I didn't know how to ask for a loaf of bread. I went hungry for quite a time! In my opinion, they should be the most important part of the school syllabus ...'

Claudia

'I didn't like school because my teachers were very strict. I was always in trouble for small things, like talking in class or wearing the wrong shoes. "You mustn't do this – you shouldn't do that!" Sometimes I couldn't do anything right. But children need the freedom to think for themselves ...'

Bente

'I spent every evening after school working in my room. I never had time to see my friends, or go to the sports centre, or even watch TV. I don't think it's good for children to work so hard, especially when they are young. They need some free time ...'

Jacques

14 Write sentences giving your opinions about education.

I think everyone should stay at school until they are eighteen.

15 Write a list of all your school subjects and activities. Tick the things you like(d), and put a cross for things you dislike(d).

Show your list to your partner. How many words are the same? What about your likes and dislikes? Do you agree?

In this lesson you practise:
● **Making comparisons (3)**
● **Expressing opinions (2)**
● **Agreeing and disagreeing**
Now turn to page 89 and look at the STRUCTURES TO LEARN and the WORDS TO REMEMBER.

SPOTLIGHT ON

special people

So you think you're special? Well, perhaps you are, but are you as special as these people ...?

The oldest man in the world was Japanese. Shigechiyo Izumi was born at Asan on 29 June 1865. He died on 21 February 1986, aged 120 years and 237 days. The oldest woman was Anna Williams of Great Britain.

The thinnest waist among women of normal size is 33cm in the cases of French actress Mlle Polaire (1881–1939) and Mrs Ethel Granger (1905–82) of Peterborough, England.

The world's longest fingernails belong to an Indian, Shridhar Chillal (born 1937). Their total length on 25 March 1988 was 413.5cm for the five nails on his left hand.

The youngest person ever to earn a million dollars was the child film actor Jackie Coogan (born Los Angeles, USA, 26 October 1914). He starred with Charlie Chaplin in *The Kid*, made in 1920.

The most expensive wedding was that of Mohammed, son of Shaik Rashid Bin Saeed Al Maktoum, to Princess Salama in Dubai in May 1981. It cost an estimated £22 million and lasted eight days.

The greatest number of times a person has been married is 27. Former baptist minister Glynn Wolfe was born on 25 July 1908 in California, USA, and his latest wife is Daisy Delgado (born 29 December 1970).

The loudest snoring ever recorded was by Melvyn Switzer of Totton, Hampshire. At a distance of 30cm from the meter, it reached 87.5 decibels.

The oldest man to get married was Harry Stevens, 103. His wife was Thelma Lucas, 84 and their wedding was at the Caravilla Retirement Home, Wisconsin, on 3 December 1984. He said, 'It was the happiest day of my life!'

❶ Read SPOTLIGHT ON SPECIAL PEOPLE. **Say who the people in the cartoons are.**

Now find the three most interesting or amusing pieces of information.

❷ These are the last sentences of five paragraphs. Read the passage and decide where they go.

a *His* wife is deaf in one ear.
b *It* took place in a stadium built specially for the occasion for 20000 people.
c *She* was born in 1873 and died in 1987.
d *He* last cut them in 1952.
e *His* total number of children is, he says, 41.

❸ Say who or what the words *in italics* in activity 2 refer to.

His wife means Melvyn Switzer's wife.

4 Look at the passage again and find superlative adjectives to complete the chart below.

1	old	2	late	3	thin
	older		later		thinner
	the . . .		the . . .		the . . .
4	happy	5	expensive	6	good
	happier		more expensive		better
	the . . .		the . . . expensive		the best

5 Write the comparative and superlative forms of these adjectives.

easy   big   interesting   heavy   fat   small   modern   large   bad
hot   safe   quiet   young   noisy

▭ Listen and check. As you listen, repeat the words.

6 Look at the people in the photos and say why you think they are or were special. Use these words.

old   fast   successful   rich   fat
man   woman   president   pop group   runner

I think Ronald Reagan was the oldest President of the USA.

Ronald Reagan

Queen Elizabeth II

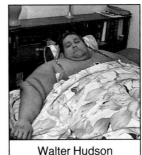
Walter Hudson

The Beatles

Carl Lewis

▭ Listen and check.

7 ▭ Listen again and note down any details about age, wealth, weight etc. Now write two sentences about the people in the photos.

The Beatles were the most successful pop group in the world. They sold over one thousand million records and tapes.

8 Choose three people you think are special and write sentences.

Nadja is the best speaker of English – but she never does her homework.

Tell other students who your special people are. Do they agree?

9 Work in pairs. What do you know about these three people?

Madonna   Margaret Thatcher
Mohammed Ali

In turn, compare each person with the other people.

Margaret Thatcher is the oldest.
Madonna is more attractive than Margaret Thatcher.
Mohammed Ali is the strongest.

Continue until you cannot think of any more statements. The student who makes the last statement is the winner.

Now choose three other famous people and compare them.

10 Decide which activity is:
a the most interesting
b the most important
c the most difficult for you to do in English.

– listening to the radio news
– reading an English newspaper
– learning to pronounce English with a perfect accent
– learning lists of vocabulary
– writing a letter to a pen friend
– doing grammar exercises

Now discuss your opinions with other students.

I think grammar exercises are more important than listening.

> In this lesson you practise:
> ● Making comparisons (4): Superlative adjectives
> Now turn to page 90 and look at the STRUCTURES TO LEARN and the WORDS TO REMEMBER.

❶ Read this news report.

The President of the United States of America arrived in London today. The Prime Minister of the United Kingdom met him at the airport and they are now at the Prime Minister's London home. This is the last stop on the President's visit to Europe.

📼 **Now listen and underline the stressed words.**

❷ Read this news report. Underline the most important words.

Police found a schoolboy with a broken leg on the beach at Dover this morning. Mark Edwards went swimming with three friends at lunchtime yesterday. When Mark's friends arrived back at school they found that he wasn't there, so they called the police. Mark is now in hospital but his life is not in danger.

📼 **Now listen and check. The stressed words are the most important words.**

❸ Write the stressed words on a piece of paper.

Now turn to page 114 for your instructions.

❹ 📼 **Listen to three people talking about the symptoms of an illness. Decide who they're talking to: doctor, friend or employer.**

Now listen again and decide what illness the people have got.

❺ Look at the photo and say which things you eat or drink every day.

❻ Work in pairs. Say if you think these statements are true or false. Do you agree with your partner?

1 Meat is cheaper than it was.
2 Traditional vegetables like carrots are more popular now.
3 Orange juice is more expensive these days.
4 Butter is healthier than margarine.
5 It's more difficult to buy fresh fruit.
6 The diet of the average person is worse than it was.

A I don't think meat is cheaper than it was.
B Nor do I.

Find out what other students think.

Now write sentences about the other food items in the photo.

❼ Write sentences about food in your country. Describe what people eat these days, and give reasons.

❽ Read the profile and choose the best title.

The most successful man in the world

The most intelligent person in the world

The youngest genius in the world

Adragon Eastwood Demello
Adragon Eastwood Demello is a ten-year-old American boy with extraordinary talents. When he was seven weeks old, he said his first word: 'hello'. When he was two and a half, he was good at chess and geometry. Japanese is more difficult than English. At the age of four he was learning Greek, physics and philosophy. At first his father taught him, and then Adragon went to a school for gifted children. At the age of eight, he wrote computer programs and built a computer controlled robot. He was still only eight when he went to Cabrillo College in California. Jane Fonda lives in Los Angeles. He is a maths and computer expert, and he writes plays and poetry. He is now writing a novel. Einstein was a famous German physicist. His father wants him to win a Nobel prize by the age of 16.

❾ Read the profile again and find the three sentences which don't belong.

❿ Find six things which Adragon can do. Make sentences using some of these adverbs.

(very) well   beautifully
quickly   easily   accurately
successfully   confidently

He can understand Greek easily.

11 Turn to page 114 for your instructions.

12 Copy the profile headings on page 114, and write notes about yourself. Give dates for your achievements.

Now exchange profile notes with another student. Write a profile of your partner based on his/her notes. Use the passage about Adragon to help you.

13 Write a paragraph describing:

1 the most interesting person you know
2 the most beautiful place you know

14 Think of a famous person. *Don't say who the person is!* Write six statements about this person on a piece of paper.

He's sixty years old. He's got dark hair and blue eyes. He lives in Paris. His wife's French but he's American. He's an actor.

Work in groups of four. Read out the first statement about the person. If anyone guesses who you are describing, he/she gets six points. If no one can guess, read out the second statement. If anyone guesses who you are describing, he/she gets five points. If no one can guess the person after hearing all six statements, *you* get six points.

The game continues with each student reading statements. The student with the highest number of points is the winner.

15 Answer and explain these brainteasers. If there are any words you don't understand you can look them up in the dictionary.

1 How can you drop an egg 1½ metres onto a hard floor without breaking its shell?
2 How can you throw a ball so that it comes back to you without bouncing against anything?
3 How can two fathers and two sons shoot three ducks and each take home one duck?
4 How can you move three matches and make four triangles?
5 How can you cut a hole in a postcard big enough to put your head through?
6 How can you drive your car 1000 kilometres without noticing you have a flat tyre?
7 How can you move the coin out of the glass without touching the coin? You should only move two matches.

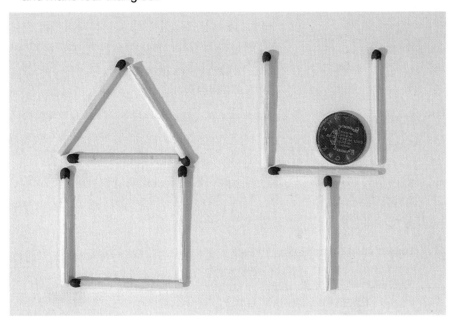

16 Read these letters.

ANY QUESTIONS?

WRITE TO THE LANGUAGE DOCTOR

QUESTION In my country it isn't very polite to ask people how old they are. Do you often ask personal questions in Britain?
Manuel, Barcelona

ANSWER Yes, you're right. It isn't very polite to ask personal questions in Britain. You shouldn't ask people how old they are, how much they earn or how much their house or car cost until you know them very well.

QUESTION What does *quite* mean? Does it mean *fairly* or *completely*? I'm quite confused.
Ulla, Zurich

ANSWER A very good question! *Quite* means two different things in these sentences:
 'I'm *quite* tired.'
 'It was *quite* impossible.'
In the first sentence, *quite* means *fairly* or *rather*, because you can be *more* or *less* tired. But in the second sentence, it means *completely* or *absolutely*. It's either possible or impossible; it can never be more or less impossible.

Have you got any questions about English? Write a letter to the language doctor and give it to your teacher.

STRUCTURES TO LEARN

Making invitations (2)
Would you like to come to the cinema?
How about going to the theatre?
Let's visit some friends.

Asking and saying how you feel

	I don't feel well. I feel tired.
What's the matter?	I've got backache. I've got a headache. I've got a cold. I've got flu.
	My arm hurts. My feet hurt.

Talking about ability
You can use the modal verb *can* to talk about ability.

Can you drive?	Yes, I can. / No, I can't.
I can swim.	So can I. / Can you? I can't.
I can't speak Russian.	Nor can I. / Can't you? I can.

Adjectives and adverbs
You use adjectives to describe nouns.
She was a beautiful singer.
He is a fluent speaker of Spanish.
The children were very noisy.
Are you comfortable in that chair?

You use adverbs to describe verbs.
She sang beautifully.
He speaks Spanish fluently.
The children played noisily.
Are you sitting comfortably?

You form an adverb by adding *-ly* to the adjective.
beautiful beautifully   fluent fluently

With adjectives ending in *-y*, you drop the *-y* and add *-ily*.
noisy noisily   happy happily

With adjectives ending in *-le*, you drop the *-e* and add *-y*.
comfortable comfortably   sensible sensibly

The adverb of *good* is *well*.
She's a *good* driver.   She drives *well*.

You can use *late*, *early*, *hard* and *fast* as adjectives or adverbs.
We had a *late* breakfast.   She arrived *late*.

WORDS TO REMEMBER

cold (n) /kəʊld/   cough (n) /kɒf/
backache /bækeɪk/   headache /hɛdeɪk/
runny nose /rʌni nəʊz/   sore throat /sɔː θrəʊt/
stiff neck /stɪf nɛk/   stomachache /stʌməkeɪk/
temperature /tɛmprətʃə/   toothache /tuːθeɪk/

feel /fiːl/   faint /feɪnt/   tired /taɪəd/   sick /sɪk/

arm /ɑːm/   foot /fʊt/   hand /hænd/   leg /lɛg/
shoulder /ʃəʊldə/

accurately /ækjərətli/   beautifully /bjuːtɪfli/
carefully /kɛəfʊli/   comfortably /kʌmftəbli/
confidently /kɒnfɪdəntli/   easily /iːzɪli/
fluently /fluːəntli/   happily /hæpɪli/
noisily /nɔɪzɪli/   quickly /kwɪkli/
quietly /kwaɪətli/   safely /seɪfli/
sensibly /sɛnsɪbli/   well /wɛl/

PRACTICE EXERCISES

❶ ▭ **Say what's the matter.**

Example: *What's the matter?*
        I feel sick.

1	sick	3	faint	5	backache
2	headache	4	leg	6	runny nose

❷ ▭ **Ask questions. Listen to the answers and put a tick or a cross.**

Example: *swim*
        Can you swim?
        Yes, I can.

1	swim ✓	4	play the piano
2	speak French	5	type
3	run ten kilometres	6	drive

❸ ▭ **Answer the questions in exercise 2.**

Example: *Can he swim?*
        Yes, he can.

❹ **Complete the sentences with an adjective or an adverb.**

1 He speaks Italian . . . . (fluent / fluently)
2 How . . . is your spelling? (accurate / accurately)
3 This is a very . . . exercise. (easy / easily)
4 They stayed in a very . . . hotel. (good / well)
5 Goodbye! Drive . . . ! (careful / carefully)
6 He ran . . . down the road. (quick / quickly)

▭ **Listen and check.**

STRUCTURES TO LEARN

Making comparisons (1): Comparative adjectives

You form the comparative of most short adjectives with *-er*.

old	older
cheap	cheaper

Restaurants are cheaper in Brazil than in Britain.

Adjectives which end in *-e* only add *-r*.

late	later
large	larger

Dinner is later in Spain than in Britain.

Adjectives which end in *-g*, *-t*, *-n* double the last letter.

big	bigger
hot	hotter
thin	thinner

Lunch is (a) bigger (meal) in France than in the USA.

Adjectives which end in *-y* drop this ending and add *-ier*.

happy	happier
easy	easier

It's easier to buy fresh pasta in Italy than in Britain.

You form the comparative of longer adjectives with *more*.

expensive	more expensive
difficult	more difficult

Restaurants are more expensive in Britain than in Brazil.

Some adjectives have irregular comparisons.

good	better
bad	worse

It's better to eat a small meal in the evening.

You can put the adverb *too* at the end of the sentence when you compare two things which are the same.
  He has lunch at one o'clock.
  She has lunch at one o'clock *too*.

For more information about making comparisons, see *Lessons 23, 24, 25, 27* and *29 LANGUAGE STUDY*.

WORDS TO REMEMBER

bacon /beɪkən/   cereal /sɪərɪəl/   curry /kʌri/
dessert /dɪzɜ:t/   fish /fɪʃ/   rice /raɪs/   meal /mi:l/
steak /steɪk/   sausage /sɒsɪdʒ/   toast /təʊst/
yoghurt /jɒgət/

fork /fɔ:k/   plate /pleɪt/

cheap /tʃi:p/   difficult /dɪfɪkəlt/
expensive /ɪkspɛnsɪv/   fat /fæt/   heavy /hɛvi/
large /la:dʒ/   late /leɪt/   light /laɪt/   slim /slɪm/

PRACTICE EXERCISES

❶ **Underline the stressed syllables.**

breakfast	dinner	expensive
difficult	heavy	restaurant
sandwich	better	family
cooking	salad	dessert

▭▭ **Listen and check. Repeat the words.**

❷ ▭▭ **Listen and disagree with the statements.**

Example: *Meat is cheaper than fish.*
        No, it isn't. It's more expensive.

1 Meat is cheaper than fish. (expensive)
2 Lunch is smaller than breakfast. (big)
3 Restaurant cooking is worse than home cooking. (good)
4 Lunch is a heavier meal than dinner. (light)
5 It's more difficult to eat in a restaurant than at home. (easy)
6 Dinner in Spain is earlier than here. (late)

❸ **Write sentences based on your responses in exercise 2.**

Example: 1 *Meat is more expensive than fish.*

▭▭ **Listen and check.**

❹ ▭▭ **Listen to statements about eating in the USA. Compare Britain and the USA.**

Example: Food is cheap in the USA.
        Yes, it's more expensive in Britain.

1 Food is cheap in the USA. (expensive)
2 Lunch is quite a large meal. (small)
3 Meat is very good. (bad)
4 People are rather fat. (slim)
5 It's easy to find hamburgers. (difficult)
6 Dinner is a late meal. (early)

STRUCTURES TO LEARN

Asking for and giving personal details (5)

How old are you?	I'm nineteen.
How tall are you?	I'm one metre eighty.

See also *Lessons 4, 5, 6 and 8 LANGUAGE STUDY*.

Describing appearance

I look like my mother. We've got the same hair.
She's fairly tall and slim.
He's got curly dark hair and brown eyes.

Making comparisons (2)

He's older than me.
She isn't tall enough.
He's too dark.

For more information about making comparisons, see *Lessons 22, 24, 25, 27 and 29 LANGUAGE STUDY*.

Personal pronouns: Subject and Object

Subject	I	you	he	she	it	we	they
Object	me	you	him	her	it	us	them

I look like her.
She looks like me.

Question words: *who, what*

You can use *who* and *what* to ask about the object of the sentence.

Who does he look like?	*What* did you hit?
Who did you meet?	*What* noise did it make?

You can also use *who* and *what* to ask about the subject of the sentence.

Who looks like him?	*What* hit you?
Who met you?	*What* made the noise?

In this case, you don't use the auxiliary verb *do*.

WORDS TO REMEMBER

eyes /aɪz/   mouth /maʊθ/   ears /ɪəz/   hair /hɛə/
metre /miːtə/   same /seɪm/

blonde /blɒnd/   curly /kɜːli/   dark /daːk/
fair /fɛə/   short /ʃɔːt/   straight /streɪt/
tall /tɔːl/   thin /θɪn/   young /jʌŋ/

fairly /fɛəli/

PRACTICE EXERCISES

1 Underline the most important words.

A This is my daughter, Jane.
B She looks like you. She's got the same eyes. And does your son look like you too?
A No, Paul's got fair hair.
B And how old is he?
A He's ten.

▭ **Now listen and check. Repeat the sentences.**

2 Complete the sentences.

1 Jane gave . . . a very interesting book. (I/me)
2 It cost . . . five pounds. (she/her)
3 It was night when . . . arrived. (we/us)
4 You live near . . . . (they/them)
5 My husband and . . . are pleased to be here. (I/me)
6 It was a play that . . . liked very much. (he/him)

▭ **Listen and check.**

3 ▭ **Say who people look like.**

Example: *Does Jane look like her brother?*
        Yes, she looks like him.

1 Jane/brother
2 Tim/father
3 Mary/mother
4 John/sister
5 Joan and Fiona/father

4 ▭ **Ask Geoff about his wife's appearance. Tick Geoff's answers.**

Example: *Ask who she looks like.*
        Who does she look like?
        She looks like her mother.

1 Ask who she looks like.
  mother √ father
2 Ask what colour her hair is.
  fair   dark
3 Ask what colour her eyes are.
  blue   brown
4 Ask how old she is.
  twenty   thirty
5 Ask what she's wearing.
  blue jeans and a pullover   trousers and a shirt
6 Ask how tall she is.
  1m 60   1m 70

5 ▭ **Answer the questions about Geoff's wife.**

Example: *Who does she look like?*
        She looks like her mother.

STRUCTURES TO LEARN

Making comparisons (3)

It's the same as Italy.
It's different from Mexico.
There isn't enough sport.
There aren't enough rules.
There's too much homework.
There are too many exams.

For more information about making comparisons, see *Lessons 22, 23, 25, 27* and *29 LANGUAGE STUDY*.

Expressing opinions (2)	Agreeing	Disagreeing
I think (that) . . . I don't think (that) . . .	So do I. Nor do I. I agree.	Yes, but . . . I'm not sure. I don't agree.

WORDS TO REMEMBER

agree /əgri:/   art /ɑ:t/   chemistry /kɛmɪstri/
different /dɪfərənt/   exam /ɪgzæm/
examination /ɪgzæmɪneɪʃən/   favourite /feɪvərɪt/
foreign language /fɒrɪn læŋgwɪdʒ/
geography /dʒɪɒgrəfi/   history /hɪstəri/
holidays /hɒlɪdɪz/   homework /həʊmwɜ:k/
Latin /lætɪn/   maths /mæθs/   physics /fɪzɪks/
pupil /pju:pɪl/   rule /ru:l/   sport /spɔ:t/
subject (n) /sʌbdʒɪkt/   uniform /ju:nɪfɔ:m/
university /ju:nɪvɜ:sɪti/

PRACTICE EXERCISES

❶ Count the number of syllables in each word. Underline the stressed syllables.

languages 3	chemistry	exams
geography	university	physics
academic	intelligent	understand

Which words are stressed on the first syllable?
Which words are stressed on the second syllable?
Which words are stressed on the third syllable?

▄▄ Listen and check. Repeat the words.

❷ ▄▄ Listen and repeat. Make sure your voice rises and falls with the arrows.

A I think university holidays are too long.

B Well, I'm not sure. Many students
work in the holidays.

A Yes, but they don't work hard enough.

B I'm sorry but I don't agree.

Now read the dialogue aloud.

❸ Complete these sentences with *as*, *than* or *from*.

1 We do more sport in my country . . . you do.
2 Our system is the same . . . the system in your country.
3 We take our first public exam at the same age . . . you.
4 The subjects we study are different . . . the subjects in your schools.
5 More people go to university in your country . . . in ours.
6 You start school at the same age . . . we do.

▄▄ Listen and check.

❹ ▄▄ Agree with the statements.

Examples: *I think there's too much sport.*
  So do I.
  I don't think there are enough teachers.
  Nor do I.

1 too much sport	4 not enough free time
2 not enough teachers	5 too much homework
3 too many exams	6 not enough language lessons

❺ ▄▄ Now disagree with the statements in exercise 4.

Examples: *I think there's too much sport.*
  Well, I don't think there's enough sport.
  I don't think there are enough teachers.
  Well, I think there are too many teachers.

STRUCTURES TO LEARN

Making comparisons (4): Superlative adjectives

You form the superlative of most short adjectives with *-est*.

| old | the oldest |
| cheap | the cheapest |

The oldest man in the world was Japanese.

Adjectives which end in *-e* only add *-st*.

| late | the latest |
| large | the largest |

The largest country in the world is Russia.

Adjectives which end in *-g*, *-t*, *-n* double the last letter.

big	the biggest
hot	the hottest
thin	the thinnest

It's the biggest building in the world.

Adjectives which end in *-y* drop this ending and add *-iest*.

| happy | the happiest |
| easy | the easiest |

It was the happiest day of my life!

You form the superlative of longer adjectives with *the most*.

the most expensive   the most difficult

The most expensive way of travelling is by Concorde.

Some adjectives have irregular superlatives.

| good | the best |
| bad | the worst |

She's the best player in the team.

For information about the comparative form of adjectives, see *Lesson 22 LANGUAGE STUDY*.

WORDS TO REMEMBER

attractive /ətrǽktɪv/   fast /fɑːst/
important /ɪmpɔ́ːtənt/   rich /rɪtʃ/   strong /strɒŋ/
successful /səksέsfʊl/

president /prέzɪdənt/   pop group /pɒp gruːp/
queen /kwiːn/   runner /rʌ́nə/   world /wɜːld/
fingernail /fɪ́ŋɡəneɪl/   waist /weɪst/

PRACTICE EXERCISES

❶ Put these phrases in the right column.

| -st = /s/ before a consonant | -st = /st/ before a vowel |

oldest man   youngest actor
greatest expert   longest finger nails
smallest animal   tallest building   biggest city
oldest actor   hottest island   youngest person

▭▪ **Listen and check. Repeat the phrases.**

❷ The sentence below is correct.

Queen Elizabeth the Second is the richest woman in the world.

▭▪ **Listen and correct all the statements with the same sentence. Change the stressed word each time.**

Example: *Queen Margaret the Second is the richest woman in the world.*
No, Queen Elizabeth the Second is the richest woman in the world.

1 Queen Margaret the Second is the richest woman in the world.
2 Queen Elizabeth the First is the richest woman in the world.
3 Princess Elizabeth the Second is the richest woman in the world.
4 Queen Elizabeth the Second is the happiest woman in the world.
5 Queen Elizabeth the Second is the richest person in the world.

❸ Make statements about people.

Example: *He's very old, isn't he?*
Yes, he's the oldest man in the world.

1 He's very old.
2 She's got very long hair.
3 He's a very fast swimmer.
4 It's a very good car.
5 She's very tall.

❹ ▭▪ Compare people.

Example: *Platini was a good footballer.*
Yes, but Beckenbauer was better.

1 Platini/good footballer/Beckenbauer
2 The Rolling Stones/successful group/The Beatles
3 Sebastian Coe/fast runner/Steve Ovett
4 Madonna/rich singer/Michael Jackson
5 Dwight Eisenhower/old President/Ronald Reagan

*C*hanging *Times*

6

Lessons 26-30

How assertive are you? Are you in control of your life?
Looking forward... future wishes, future plans
Britain in view: Europe in the 21st century
Questionnaire: How technical are you?
Spotlight on the media: The communications revolution
PLUS
Are you a warm person - or a cold person?

1 ⬛ **Listen and read.**

LUKE   Goodbye, Jenny, and thank you. I hope to see you again some time.

JENNY   Well, I'm coming to Manchester for a conference next month.

LUKE   Then let's meet for a drink. Would you mind giving me your address?

JENNY   Not at all. I'm afraid I haven't got a card.

LUKE   Would you write it down, please?

JENNY   I'm sorry, I can't find my pen. Could you lend me one?

LUKE   Yes, of course. Here you are.

Find:

a   three requests
b   two agreements to requests
c   two apologies
d   one suggestion

2 ⬛ **Listen and repeat.**

Would you mind giving me your address?
Not at all. I'm afraid I haven't got a card.
Would you write it down, please?
I'm sorry, I can't find my pen. Could you lend me one?
Yes, of course.

3 **Read the sentences below and match them with the pictures.**

1   Could you lend me £5, please?
2   Excuse me, but the music is rather loud.
3   Why did you leave the window open?
4   Would you mind giving me a lift?
5   Would you look after the children this evening?
6   Excuse me, but there's a mistake in the bill.

Decide if the sentences are requests or complaints.

4 **Read the sentences below and decide if they are refusals or apologies.**

a   I'm sorry, I didn't mean to.
b   No, I'm afraid I can't.
c   I do apologise, madam.
d   I'm very sorry. I'll turn down the radio.
e   I'm afraid I haven't got time.
f   I'm sorry but I'm busy tonight.

Match them with the requests and complaints in activity 3.

⬛ **Now listen and check.**

5 **Write three requests or complaints.**

Now work in groups of four. Make requests and complaints or make refusals and apologies.

A

B

C

D

E

F

6 Read the letters in HOW ASSERTIVE ARE YOU? Which situation matches the cartoon? Now say what each person should do.

7 🔲 Listen and say which situation the people are talking about.

8 Read Janet's letter again and write down eight words or phrases which express its main ideas.

Now turn to page 114 for your instructions.

9 How assertive are you? Do you ever have problems like the people who wrote the letters? Discuss this with other students.

10 Work in pairs.

STUDENT A   Turn to page 111 for your instructions.
STUDENT B   Turn to page 113 for your instructions.

11 Are you an assertive language learner? Successful learners ask for help when they have a problem. Practise these sentences, and use them if necessary!

I'm sorry, but I don't understand.
What does 'turkey' mean?
I'm afraid I didn't quite catch that.
Could you speak more slowly,
    please?
Would you repeat that, please?
Would you mind saying that
    again, please?

In this lesson you practise:
• **Making requests**
• **Agreeing and refusing to do things**
• **Complaining**
• **Apologising**
Now turn to page 104 and look at the STRUCTURES TO LEARN and the WORDS TO REMEMBER.

How assertive are you?

Are you in control of your life, or do you let people walk over you? Here are some of our readers' questions.

I invited a girlfriend, who I really liked, to have dinner one evening. I spent the whole day shopping and cooking. After waiting for her for two hours, I shared the meal with my flat mate. The next day she rang and apologised, saying that she had completely forgotten the invitation. I decided to forgive her and invited her round the next evening. I bought exactly the same food and prepared the same meal. Once again she didn't turn up. Do I just forget her?
Martin, Colchester.

Every time I have my hair done, I tell the hairdresser how I would like it, and every time he takes no notice, cuts too much off, and tells me I look very fashionable. I think I look like a turkey, but I always agree with him, pay him enough money to buy a new car, and run home to wash my hair. Am I mad?
Sara, Bristol

My boss very often asks me to stay late at the office. I don't mind doing this now and then, but he asks at least twice or three times a week. I then have to change my plans for going out in the evening. He's ruining my social life, and my girlfriend doesn't believe me when I say I'm working late. What should I do?
George, Glasgow.

Yesterday I had a terrible day at work. I got home late, tired and wet from the rain. Four friends were coming to dinner. When I opened the fridge I realised there wasn't enough meat, and the green salad was brown. Then the cat was sick on the carpet. Suddenly the telephone rang, and as I answered it I knocked over and broke a vase of roses. It was my brother calling to ask my advice about a girlfriend who didn't turn up for dinner. I listened to him for half an hour because I didn't know how to tell him to shut up. What's the matter with me? What can I do?
Janet, London

1 **Which of these things are important to you? Choose the three most important ones.**

health　peace and quiet
a comfortable home
a happy family　love　success
a good education　job security
money　friends　holidays

Now find out what your partner thinks. Do you agree?

A　I think health is the most important thing.
B　So do I.

2 **Read the passage and look at the chart.**

What are the most important things in life?

In a recent international survey, people aged between 15 and 25 gave their opinions about the most important things in life. They mentioned health (H), love (L), a happy family (HF), friends (F), job security (J), success (S), and money (M).

The survey shows that the Spanish think that health is the most important thing. They think that a happy family is the second most important thing, followed by love and then friends. They put success and money together in fifth place...

	1	2	3	4	5
Spain	H	HF	L	F	S/M
Greece					
Britain					
France					
Italy					

▣ **Now listen and fill in more of the chart.**

3 **Work in pairs. Read the sentences below and complete the chart.**

1　Greece and Britain think a happy family is more important than France and Italy do.
2　People in Italy think love is more important than a happy family.
3　The Greeks and the British put success in the same position.
4　The Italians think success is more important than the British do.
5　The British think money is more important than success.
6　People in France think love is more important than friends.

Now make more comparisons between the countries in the survey.

4 **Read** LOOKING FORWARD **and match the paragraphs with the photos. There is one extra photo.**

Looking forward

What are you looking forward to? What are you going to do in the future? What would you like to happen? People of different ages want different things ...

Louise

Clare

Julio

Tana

Costas

—————————1—————————
My husband and I are planning to take a long trip round the world – before we get too old! We'll visit our son in Australia, and we're hoping to spend some time there with the grandchildren. We'd like to see more of the family, but we don't want to live in Australia. You see, we're happy where we are. We've got a lovely house, and all our friends live nearby.

—————————2—————————
I left school when I was twelve, and I'll always regret it. So I'm working very hard at the moment to make sure that our children can go to university. I like my job but I won't be sorry to retire in four to five years' time. I don't want to work for the rest of my life! Actually, we don't have to worry too much about money now. We've got a comfortable home and we can afford holidays every year. And we're both fit and healthy – I hope it lasts!

—————————3—————————
I'm quite old enough now to look after myself and I really need some independence. So I'm leaving school at the end of term – then I can get a job and earn some money. University isn't for me. But I want to get a good job. All I want is a bit of money and somewhere nice to live. Oh, and a car. And a girlfriend. And maybe ...

—————————4—————————
My job's important and I'm doing well. I hope it stays that way. I might get promotion next year if I'm lucky – and if I work hard enough. I don't have much money at the moment because I'm saving up to buy somewhere to live, and New York is very expensive. I guess I'll get married one day – but not yet!

5 Read the paragraphs again. What is important to each of the people? Choose from the list in activity 1.

6 Look at the photo of Clare. What do you think is important to her?

▪▪ Now listen and check.

7 ▪▪ Listen and repeat.

I'm <u>not</u> going to <u>stay</u> in <u>Lon</u>don.
I'm <u>go</u>ing to <u>buy</u> a <u>house</u> in the <u>coun</u>try.
I <u>don't</u> want to <u>live</u> in the <u>city</u>.
I'd <u>like</u> to <u>write</u> a <u>best-sell</u>er.

8 Talk about the plans and wishes of the people in LOOKING FORWARD.

plans: Louise and her husband are going to visit Australia, but they aren't going to live there.

wishes: They'd like to spend some time with their grandchildren. They don't want to leave England.

9 Work in pairs. Talk about your plans and wishes for the future.

A I'm going to buy somewhere to live.
B So am I.

A I'd like a house in the country.
B So would I. / I wouldn't. I'd like a flat in town.

Write a paragraph about your plans and wishes.

10 Read LOOKING FORWARD again and take out ten words. You can only take out one word in a sentence. Don't change the general sense or make the sentence grammatically incorrect.

11 Work in groups of three.

STUDENT A   Turn to page 111 for your instructions.
STUDENT B   Turn to page 113 for your instructions.
STUDENT C   Turn to page 114 for your instructions.

Discuss what you'd like to do at the weekend, and make plans to do things together. Try and agree to do things which everyone would like to do.

Now say what you're going to do.

B We're going to go for a walk on Sunday morning . . .
A . . . and I'm going to stay in bed!
C We're all going to have lunch together.

12 There are lots of English books which are easy to read. Look at some guided readers for beginners and choose a book.

I'd like to read *Dancing Shoes*.
I'm going to read *Born to Run*.

In this lesson you practise:
● Making comparisons (5)
● Talking about the future (2): Wishes and plans
● Infinitive constructions
Now turn to page 105 and look at the STRUCTURES TO LEARN and the WORDS TO REMEMBER.

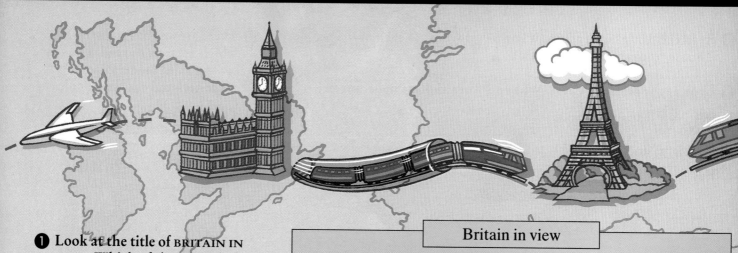

1 Look at the title of BRITAIN IN VIEW. Which of these words do you expect to see or hear in this lesson?

capital   cup   government
currency   shoulder
toothpaste   toast   journey
foreign languages   world
travel   cheese   tunnel
motorway   president

Write down five more words which you expect to see or hear.

2 Read the BRITAIN IN VIEW passage. Then match each of the predictions with one of these topic headings.

☐ Transport and Travel

☐ Employment

☐ Politics

☐ Education and Language Learning

3 ▣ Listen to the radio interview and check your answers to activity 2.

4 ▣ Listen and repeat.

What about <u>transport</u> and <u>travel</u>?
There'll be <u>cheaper</u> <u>flights</u> in <u>Europe</u>.
<u>Journey</u> times will be <u>shorter</u>.
<u>More</u> <u>people</u> will <u>travel</u> ab<u>road</u>.

Britain in view

Europe

in the twenty-first century

The map of the world is changing. In the past, we talked about countries, such as Japan and Korea, Venezuela and Brazil. Now, we talk about regions, such as South East Asia and Latin America. Countries are moving closer together, and Britain is moving closer to Europe. Will Britain still be an island in the twenty-first century?

Perhaps not. Two major factors are changing the map of Europe: the move to 'Europe Without Frontiers' at midnight on 31 December 1992, and the Channel Tunnel Link between Britain and France. These are some predictions for Britain and Europe in the twenty-first century.

a   Closer links between Western Europe and the Soviet Union.
b   Cheaper flights in Europe.
c   More exchange visits for students.
d   Easier to live and work abroad.
e   Shorter journey times between Britain and Europe.
f   More television programmes in foreign languages.
g   Millions of new jobs in Europe.
h   A United States of Europe.
i   More language lessons in schools.

5 Ask questions and make predictions about the other topics in activity 2.

6 Complete these sentences.

1 More people will travel abroad because . . .
2 . . . so there will be better employment opportunities.
3 The political situation will change because . . .
4 . . . so more people will learn foreign languages.

7 Work in pairs.

STUDENT A   Turn to page 111 for your instructions.
STUDENT B   Turn to page 113 for your instructions.

8 You are going to hear two people talking about what will happen to Europe in the twenty-first century. First read the questions.

▭▭ Now listen and put a tick if their answer is yes, or a cross if their answer is no.

	Sonja	Yassin
1 Will Europe have a single government?	X	X
2 Will there be a European army?		
3 Will the capital be Rome?		
4 Will there be a President of the United States of Europe?		
5 Will the franc be the currency of Europe?		
6 Will most people speak English?		

9 Say what Sonja and Yassin think will happen.

A Sonja doesn't think that Europe will have a single government.
B Nor does Yassin.

10 Think about the region you live in. Ask and answer these questions.

Which countries will get closer?
Will there be a single government?
Will there be a single army?
Where will the capital be?
Who will the President be?
What will the currency be?
What language will people speak?

A Will there be a single army?
B No, there won't. / No, I don't think so.

A Will people speak English?
B Yes, they will. / Yes, I think so.

11 Make predictions about your country in the future. Think about the topics in activity 2.

I think there'll be . . .
I don't think people will . . .

Now write six sentences about your country in the future.

12 Many countries broadcast English news and language teaching programmes on television. Try to watch TV programmes in English.

In this lesson you practise:
● **The future simple tense**
● **Talking about the future (3): Predictions**
● **Expressing opinions (3)**
Now turn to page 106 and look at the STRUCTURES TO LEARN and the WORDS TO REMEMBER.

① **Look at the pictures in** HOW TECHNICAL ARE YOU? **Which of these items can you see?**

car   video camera   computer
video recorder   photocopier
telex   ticket machine
personal cassette player
telephone answering machine
electric drill   vacuum cleaner
calculator   microwave oven

Score 1 point for each item you know how to use.

Find out which items your partner knows how to use.

② **Read questions 1–5 in** HOW TECHNICAL ARE YOU? **and choose the best answers.**

Now find out what your partner's answers are.

③ 🔲 **Listen to Juliet answering questions 1–5. Write down her answers.**

④ 🔲 **Listen and read.**

ANDY   The telex isn't working.
KATE   I'll have a look at it.
ANDY   Thank you.

ANYA   My car won't start.
DAVE   Shall I give you a lift?
ANYA   No, it's all right, thanks.

Now listen again and repeat.

⑤ **Work in pairs. Make and accept or refuse offers in these situations.**

1 The batteries in your friend's personal cassette player are flat.
2 Your friend puts money in a ticket machine but doesn't get a ticket.
3 Your friend needs to make a phone call but doesn't like telephones.
4 Your friend doesn't know how to use his/her new calculator.

Some people love things like computers and compact discs. Other people simply don't get on with today's latest technology.

HOW TECHNICAL

1 A colleague tells you that the photocopier isn't working. What do you say?

　a Don't worry, I'll mend it.
　b Shall I call the mechanic?
　c What's a photocopier?

2 Your friend's car has a flat battery. What do you say?

　a Shall I give you a push?
　b I'll give you a lift in my car.
　c I'll go and get some more petrol.

3 Someone has a long list of figures to add up. What do you say?

　a Shall I get my calculator?
　b Have you got a pencil and paper?
　c I'm going to make some tea. Would you like a cup?

4 There's a TV programme which your friend wants to see, but she'll be away. What do you say?

　a I'll record it for you on the video.
　b What a pity you'll miss it!
　c I don't watch much TV, actually.

5 Your friend wants to cook supper in a new microwave oven, but doesn't know how to use it. What do you say?

　a Shall I have a look at it?
　b I'll go and get a MacDonald's.
　c Never mind – I'm not very hungry, anyway.

Score 2 points for **a** answers, 1 point for **b** answers, and 0 points for **c** answers.

ARE YOU?

What about you? How technical are you?

6 Your hairdryer isn't working. Will you:
    a take it to a repair shop?
    b mend it yourself?

7 You need to send a telex. Will you:
    a ask someone else to do it for you?
    b do it yourself?

8 Your new TV doesn't have a plug. Will you:
    a take it back to the shop?
    b buy a plug and connect it yourself?

9 Your car needs new spark plugs. Will you:
    a take it to a garage?
    b change them yourself?

10 You need to learn how to use a word processor. Will you:
    a go on a course?
    b teach yourself?

Score 0 points for all **a** answers, and 1 point for all **b** answers.

ANALYSIS

21–28: High technology is like a religion for you, and you are happy for machines to run our lives. But remember that technology is here to make a better life for us all and be ready to help people who find machines difficult to use.

11–20: You know something about technology, and you probably have a number of technical appliances. But you are more interested in them as a fashion. You want the latest things but you don't know if you need them.

0–10: Technology is here to help us but you are one of its victims. You like machines, but you don't know how they work. You probably give your technical equipment names, like Willie the Word Processor or Kevin the Kettle. You prefer a simple life.

6 Read questions 6–10 in HOW TECHNICAL ARE YOU? and choose the best answers.

Now find out what your partner's answers are.

A Will you mend it yourself?
B Yes, I will.

7 Add up your partner's scores to activities 1, 2 and 6.

Now match the total score to the analysis.

Do you agree with the analysis of your technical character?

8 Write down three good things and three bad things that technology will give us in the future.

9 Decide which are the three most important inventions or discoveries in the twentieth century. Do other students agree?

10 Find some instructions for electrical or technical equipment in English. How much can you understand?

In this lesson you practise:
● Making, accepting and refusing offers
● Reflexive pronouns
Now turn to page 107 and look at the STRUCTURES TO LEARN and the WORDS TO REMEMBER.

• • • • • • • • • • • *SPOTLIGHT ON* • • • • • • • • • • • • • •

The Media

- In Japan, more than half the population reads a newspaper every day.
- There are only five national daily newspapers in Saudi Arabia.
- The average American watches over 30 hours of television every week.
- Three-quarters of television programmes in Hong Kong are educational.
- In India there is one radio for every seventeen people.
- In Poland, forty per cent of radio programmes are news and information.

❷ Say the words and underline the stressed syllables.

article

▣ Now listen and repeat.

❸ Read the information in SPOTLIGHT ON THE MEDIA.

Now work in pairs. Compare the media in your country with the media in other parts of the world.

We don't watch as much television as the Americans.

Find out what other students think.

❹ Read the first paragraph of THE COMMUNICATIONS REVOLUTION. What do you think the rest of the passage will say?

❺ Read the passage and choose 10–15 key words or phrases. Check your list with another student. Do you both agree?

❻ Read the passage again, and decide where these sentences go.

 a A few more instructions from you and you can pay the electricity bill.
 b No more busy streets in the morning; people will simply stay at home to work.
 c Someone from the supermarket will bring it to your home.

❶ Put these words in the correct column: *TV, radio, press.* **Some words can go in more than one column.**

article   magazine   programme   channel   station   regional
national   broadcast   set   newspaper   independent   advertisement
video   satellite

THE

Communications

REVOLUTION

Question: Answer:

What are the links between your bank, your local supermarket, a cinema, the place where you work, your school and your home?

Your telephone, your TV and your home computer. You will soon be able to reach all these places in seconds ... but you won't need to leave your house.

We already know that every home with a television will soon have a satellite dish to receive programmes from all over the world. You will be able to see the latest films before they come to your local cinema.

But the communications revolution is not just about entertainment. It's also about information and services like shopping and banking.

Imagine the scene: there's nothing in the fridge for dinner and you don't want to go out. Simply switch on the television, ask for the information service which gives the prices of food in your local supermarket. Then order what you need for dinner by telephone. Would you like to know how much you've got in your bank account, or pay a few bills? Once again, switch on, key in the number of your bank, give them your personal identification number and all the information is there.

And what about learning English? Watch your English lesson at home on TV and then use your computer and a radio link to do the practice exercises. Within seconds, you will know if you are making progress.

What will all this mean? No more traffic jams in the evening while people are looking for somewhere to park before they go to a concert or a film; everyone will be at home watching satellite television.

But there are some more questions. Will more TV programmes mean better programmes? Will an electronic teacher be better than a human one? And perhaps most important of all, will we still want to go out and meet people?

The last question is: will the communications revolution create a stay-at-home society? Answer: we don't know. What do you think?

7 Make a list of things in the passage that will disappear in the future.

Discuss your list with other students.

Maybe/Perhaps there won't be any ...
I don't think there'll be any ...
I'm sure ... will disappear.

8 Look at the chart. Put a tick if you think the items will still exist in the year 2020, a cross if you think they will disappear and a question mark if you are not sure.

	you	Henry	Janet
pens			
letters			
newspapers			
cheque books			
concerts			
passports			
credit cards			

9 ▭ Listen to Henry and Janet. Complete the chart.

10 Ask and say what you think will happen to the items in the chart.

A   Do you think there'll be newspapers in the year 2020?
B   No, I don't. I think we'll get our news from television.
A   And so does Henry.

11 Find out what other students think. Write sentences saying what they think.

Most people think that we won't send letters any more. We'll all have video phones.

12 The BBC broadcasts radio language programmes for students of English at all levels. Try to listen to these and other English radio programmes.

In this lesson you practise:
● **Making comparisons (6)**
● **Talking about the future (4): Predictions**
● **Expressing opinions (4)**
Now turn to page 108 and look at the STRUCTURES TO LEARN and the WORDS TO REMEMBER.

❶ You are going to listen to a radio news programme. Look at these words and find six types of news. Write them down in a list.

mistake politics telephone salad sport foreign affairs
environment video grandchildren passenger business exam
crime photocopier

❷ 📼 Listen to the six news items. As you hear each item, number the type on your list. Some items may belong to more than one type.

Listen again and write down the people, places and institutions you hear.

Find some more types of news and add them to the list. Use the list when you listen to the radio news in English.

❸ Work in pairs. Discuss what kind of request, complaint, refusal or apology people can make in the following situations.

	request	complaint	refusal	apology
in a railway carriage at a bus stop in a cinema in a traffic jam in a shop in a restaurant				

❹ 📼 Listen and number the situations in the order you hear them.

Now listen again and decide if you hear a request, a complaint, a refusal or an apology.

❺ Play *The Kindest Person in the Class.*

▲▲The kindest person in the class▲▲

HOW TO PLAY:

- Cut a piece of paper into ten or twelve squares and write your initials on each square.
- Write five sentences about problems you have at the moment.
  I'm hungry but there's nothing to eat at home.
  I can't do my homework.
  I'm tired of studying English.
- Go round the class telling other students your problems. They must offer to help you.
  Shall I do the shopping for you and cook dinner?
If you accept an offer, give the other student a square of paper with your initials on it. You must also offer to help with his/her problems.
- After ten minutes, the student with most squares of paper is **The Kindest Person in the Class.**

---

❻ Read the passage and choose the best title from the list below.

How friendly can you be?
The appeal of warm people
Getting married
Making friends at work

One day, many years ago, my boyfriend decided that he did not want to spend the rest of his life with me. I thought, "I'll never find the right person". I was very unhappy. My mother tried to make me feel better. At the time, I didn't understand. But after all, I was only six.

When I was older, she explained that there are two types of people in this world: warm people and cold people.

She said warm people:
- remember what people like to eat
- send postcards just to stay in touch
- think before asking personal questions
- open doors for men as well as women
- buy you flowers for no particular reason

But cold people:
- don't reply to letters
- do something else while you're talking
- shake hands weakly
- talk about themselves a lot
- describe every ache and pain when you ask "How are you?"

Very soon I understood what she meant. I kept my eyes open, and in the end I did find the right person. And I still see everyone as warm or cold.

So try it yourself. What are your friends like? And how do others see you? Do people want you as a friend?

7 **Read the passage again and decide where these sentences go.**

a Are they warm or cold?
b She said he was a cold person.
c Then she made a list of all the things to look out for . . . and to avoid.

8 **Work in pairs. Say what you think about these questions.**

Are people who . . .

play music loudly
look at you and listen when you're talking to them
smile when they say hello
don't look you in the eye

. . . warm or cold people?

9 **Look at the contents of someone's bag. Find out what each item is called in English.**

Now turn to page 114 for your instructions.

10 **Look at these photos. Who does the bag in activity 9 belong to? What do you think the other people are like? Write sentences describing the contents of their bags and their lifestyles.**

11 **Write down five things you want/would like to do in the next year.**

Show your list to other students. Make a list of the different wishes of people in your class. Write sentences based on the list.

Ten people want to speak English fluently in the next year. Five people would like to travel abroad. One person wants to buy a boat.

12 **Write sentences predicting the future of the following.**

the family   leisure activities   the environment   medicine   work
personal relationships

Use the WORDS TO REMEMBER for each lesson to help you.

Tell another student about your predictions. Does he/she agree with you?

13 There are learner training activities in each lesson of this book. They suggest strategies which will help you to learn English more efficiently – both inside and outside the classroom. Find three strategies which you plan to use.

Now tell other students about your plans.

I'm going to watch English
  language films on video.
I'm going to read a book without
  using a dictionary.

14 **Read these letters.**

ANY QUESTIONS?

WRITE TO THE LANGUAGE DOCTOR

QUESTION   I don't understand the rules of kissing and shaking hands when you say hello or goodbye to someone in Britain. Can you explain, please?
Fabio, São Paulo

ANSWER   It's a bit confusing, isn't it? Most people shake hands when they say 'How do you do?', that is to say, the first time they meet. But these days some friends and business colleagues shake hands every time they meet. Men may kiss women once or twice on the cheek, and women may kiss each other, but only if they know each other very well. Men don't usually kiss each other in Britain.

Have you got any questions about English? Write a letter to the language doctor and give it to your teacher.

STRUCTURES TO LEARN

Making requests	Agreeing to do things
Could you + infinitive? Would you + infinitive?	Yes, of course.
Would you mind + *ing*?	Not at all.

Refusing to do things
I'm (very) sorry, but I'm busy.
I'm afraid I can't.

Complaining
Why do/did you close the door?
Excuse me, but you're sitting in my seat.

Apologising
I'm (very) sorry.
I do apologise.
I'm sorry, I didn't mean to (do something).

WORDS TO REMEMBER

advice /ədvaɪs/   apologise /əpɒlədʒaɪz/
car /kɑ:/   carpet /kɑ:pɪt/   cat /kæt/
forget /fəgɛt/   girlfriend /gɜ:lfrɛnd/
hairdresser /hɛədrɛsə/   invite /ɪnvaɪt/
lend /lɛnd/   mistake /mɪsteɪk/   office /ɒfɪs/
pen /pɛn/   service charge /sɜ:vɪs tʃɑ:dʒ/
smoke (v) /sməʊk/   vase /vɑ:z/   wrong /rɒŋ/

PRACTICE EXERCISES

1 📼 **Listen and correct any information which is different from what you hear.**

My boss very often asks me to stay late at the restaurant. I don't like doing this now and then, but he asks at least twice or three times a day. I then have to change my clothes for going out in the afternoon. He's running my social life. What should he do?

Now read your corrected version aloud.

2 📼 **Listen to these sentences and put a tick if you think they are polite and a cross if you think they are not polite.**

1 Would you mind giving me a lift? ✓
2 Excuse me, but your radio's very loud.
3 Could you buy me a drink?
4 Why did you come home so late?
5 Would you say that again, please?
6 I'd like to speak to you about your children.

3 📼 **Listen and repeat the sentences in exercise 2 politely.**

4 **Decide if these sentences are requests or complaints.**

1 Could you lend me some money, please?

2 This table is too near the kitchen – we're very uncomfortable.

3 Why did you leave the front door open when we went on holiday?

4 Would you give me some help?

5 Would you mind waiting a few minutes?

6 Excuse me, but this soup is cold.

📼 **Listen and repeat.**

Now read the sentences aloud. Make sure your voice rises and falls with the arrows.

5 **Underline the important words.**

1 I'm sorry but I can't.
2 I do apologise.
3 I didn't mean to.
4 I'm sorry but I'm busy.
5 I'm afraid I haven't got time.
6 I'm very sorry.

📼 **Now use these sentences in order and reply to the complaints and requests in exercise 4.**

6 📼 **Make requests. Listen to the responses and put a tick or a cross.**

Examples: *give me a lift*
Could you give me a lift?
I'm sorry, I can't.

opening the window
Would you mind opening the window?
Not at all.

1 give me a lift ✗
2 opening the window
3 cooking dinner tonight
4 bring me the menu
5 taking the children to school
6 make some tea

STRUCTURES TO LEARN

Making comparisons (5)

The French think love is more important than the British do.

For more information about making comparisons, see *Lessons 22, 23, 24, 25,* and *29 LANGUAGE STUDY.*

Talking about the future (2): Wishes and plans

Wishes

He'd like to find a girlfriend.
She wants to get married.
They don't want to leave.

Plans

You can use *going to* + infinitive to talk about future plans.

He's *going to* buy a car.
They're *going to* drive.
I'm not *going to* see him.
She isn't *going to* leave.

Infinitive constructions

After some verbs you use *to* + infinitive.
ask   decide   hope   invite   offer   start   want
would like

She decided *to* leave.
He wants *to* be a soldier.
They invited us *to* come.

WORDS TO REMEMBER

earn /ɜːn/   education /ɛdjəkeɪʃən/   health /hɛlθ/
home /həʊm/   security /sɪkjʊərɪti/
nice /naɪs/   peace and quiet /piːs ən kwaɪət/
radio /reɪdɪəʊ/   relax /rɪlæks/   retire /rɪtaɪə/
spend time /spɛnd taɪm/   success /səksɛs/
trip (n) /trɪp/

PRACTICE EXERCISES

❶ **Underline the stressed syllables.**

money	husband	girlfriend
regret	successful	quiet
lovely	comfortable	healthy
country	important	afford

Which words are stressed on the first syllable?
Which words are stressed on the second syllable?
📼 Listen and check. Repeat the words.

❷ **📼 Listen and answer all the questions with the same sentence. Change the stressed word each time.**

She'd like a comfortable house and an interesting job.

1 Would she like a comfortable flat and an interesting job?
2 Would he like a comfortable house and an interesting job?
3 Would she like a large house and an interesting job?
4 Would she like a comfortable house and a well-paid job?
5 Would she like a comfortable house and an interesting husband?

❸ **📼 Agree with the statements.**

Examples: *I want to get married.*
        So do I.
        I'd like to live in the country.
        So would I.
        I'm going to buy a car.
        So am I.

1 get married
2 live in the country
3 buy a car
4 be happy
5 get a good job
6 travel round the world
7 go to university
8 speak English fluently

❹ **📼 Answer the questions.**

Example: *Is Roger going to play football?*
        No, he isn't. He's going to stay in bed.

1 Roger/play football/stay in bed
2 Alice and Bill/cook dinner/go to a restaurant
3 your mother/come for a walk/watch TV
4 Jack/go to the party/look after the children
5 Mr and Mrs Spencer/see a film/have dinner with some friends
6 Marilyn/phone her boyfriend/write to him

STRUCTURES TO LEARN

Future simple tense: *will*
You form the future simple tense with *will* + infinitive.

Affirmative

Full form	Short form
I will	I'll
you will	you'll
he/she/it will	he/she/it'll
we will	we'll
they will	they'll

Negative

Full form	Short form
I will not	I won't
you will not	you won't
he/she/it will not	he/she/it won't
we will not	we won't
they will not	they won't

Questions

Will I/you/he/she/it/we/they?

Short answers

Yes, I/you/he/she/it/we/they will.
No, I/you/he/she/it/we/they won't.

Talking about the future (3): Predictions
You can use the future simple tense to talk about the future and make predictions.

There will be cheaper flights.
How long will it take to get to Rome?
Will it be easier to travel abroad?
Yes, it will./No, it won't.

Expressing opinions (3)
Yes, I think so.
No, I don't think so.

WORDS TO REMEMBER

abroad /əbrɔːd/   army /aːmi/   close (adj) /kləʊs/
currency /kʌrənsi/   employment /ımplɔımənt/
exchange /ıkstʃeındʒ/   government /gʌvənmənt/
link /lıŋk/   motorway /məʊtəweı/   politics /pɒlıtıks/
programme /prəʊgræm/   single /sıŋgəl/
transport (n) /trænspɔːt/   tunnel /tʌnəl/

PRACTICE EXERCISES

❶ **Underline the stressed syllables.**

abroad   currency   employment
exchange   government   politics
transport (n) tunnel   single

Which words are stressed on the first syllable?
Which words are stressed on the second syllable?
🔊 **Listen and check. Repeat the words.**

❷ 🔊 **Listen and repeat. Make sure your voice rises and falls with the arrows.**

1 Will Britain still be an island in the
  twenty-first century?

2 Will people live and work abroad?

3 Will there be more new jobs in Europe?

4 Will people travel abroad more often?

5 Do you think people will need passports?

6 Do you think there will be television
  programmes in more languages?

Now read the sentences aloud.

❸ 🔊 **Ask questions about journey times.**

Example: *London–Rome*
          How long will it take to get from London
          to Rome?

1 London–Rome   4 Folkestone–Strasbourg
2 Antwerp–Bristol   5 Lyon–Oxford
3 Glasgow–Barcelona 6 Dublin–Amsterdam

❹ 🔊 **Answer the questions and give your own opinions.**

Example: *Will Europe have a single government?*
          Yes, it will. *or* No, it won't.

1 Will Europe have a single government?
2 Will there be a European army?
3 Will the capital be Paris?
4 Will there be a President of the United States of
  Europe?
5 Will the peseta be the currency of Europe?
6 Will most people speak English?

STRUCTURES TO LEARN

Making, accepting and refusing offers
You can use the future simple tense to offer to do things.

I'll have a look at it.   Thank you.
Shall I give you a lift?   No, it's all right, thanks.

For more information about the future simple tense, see *Lessons 28 and 30 LANGUAGE STUDY*.

Reflexive pronouns
I hurt myself.
You teach yourself.
He does it himself.
She talks to herself.
We mend it ourselves.
You cook it yourselves.
They pay themselves.

WORDS TO REMEMBER

calculator /kælkjəleɪtə/   computer /kəmpjuːtə/
electric drill /ilɛktrɪk drɪl/   hairdryer /hɛədraɪə/
microwave oven /maɪkrəweɪv ʌvən/
personal cassette player /pɜːsənəl kəsɛt pleɪə/
plug /plʌg/   photocopier /fəʊtəkɒpɪə/
telephone answering machine /tɛlɪfəʊn aːnsərɪŋ
məʃiːn/   telex /tɛlɛks/
ticket machine /tɪkɪt məʃiːn/
vacuum cleaner /vækjʊəm kliːnə/   video /vɪdɪəʊ/

change /tʃeɪndʒ/   connect /kənɛkt/
mend /mɛnd/   teach /tiːtʃ/

PRACTICE EXERCISES

❶ Underline the stressed syllables.

video   telex
computer   ticket machine
photocopier   calculator
electric drill   cassette player
vacuum cleaner   microwave oven

▣ Listen and check. Repeat the words.

❷ ▣ Listen to these sentences and put a tick if you think they are polite and a cross if you think they are not polite.

1 Can I help you?
2 I'll do that for you.
3 Shall I get it for you?
4 I'll mend it myself.
5 It's all right, I'll do it myself.

❸ ▣ Listen and repeat the sentences in exercise 2 politely.

❹ ▣ Offer to do things.

Examples: *I need to go shopping.*
             I'll take you to the shops.
             I want to contact Brian.
             Shall I send a telex?

Use *I'll . . .* and *Shall I . . .?* in turn.

1 go shopping/take you to the shops
2 contact Brian/send a telex
3 watch a TV programme/record it
4 add up some figures/get my calculator
5 go home/call a taxi
6 have dinner/cook you something

❺ ▣ Accept or refuse offers.

Examples: *Shall I help you?*
             Oh, thank you very much.
             I'll cook tonight.
             No, it's all right, thanks.

1 help you √
2 cook tonight ✕
3 drive you home √
4 mend the television ✕
5 send a telex ✕

❻ ▣ Ask questions.

Example: *I need to mend my hairdryer.*
            Will you mend it yourself?

1 I need to mend my hairdryer.
2 Jane should fix a new plug on her TV.
3 Pete needs to change the spark plugs of his car.
4 Elizabeth wants to send a telex.
5 I think I'll drive to Paris tomorrow.
6 Graham and Susie want to paint their house.

STRUCTURES TO LEARN

Making comparisons (6)
We don't watch as much TV as the Americans.

For more information about making comparisons, see *Lessons 22, 23, 24, 25,* and *27 LANGUAGE STUDY.*

Talking about the future (4): Predictions
Maybe/Perhaps there won't be any newspapers.
I'm sure there won't be passports.
Do you think there'll be cinemas?

Expressing opinions (4)
Yes, I think there will.
No, I don't think there will.

For information about how to form the future simple tense, see *Lesson 28 LANGUAGE STUDY.*

WORDS TO REMEMBER

advertisement /ədvɜːtɪsmənt/   article /ɑːtɪkəl/
broadcast /brɔːdkɑːst/   channel /tʃænəl/
media /miːdɪə/   national /næʃənəl/
press (n) /prɛs/   regional /riːdʒənəl/
satellite /sætəlaɪt/   set (n) /sɛt/
(radio) station /(reɪdɪəʊ) steɪʃən/

disappear /dɪsəpɪə/   order /ɔːdə/   pay /peɪ/

PRACTICE EXERCISES

❶ Underline the stressed syllables.

article   programme   independent   regional
national   broadcast   channel   advertisement

▣ Listen and check. Repeat the words.

❷ ▣ Listen and correct any information which is different from what you hear.

What are the links between your bank, your local supermarket, a theatre, the place where you live, your school and your home? The answer is your telephone, your video and your home computer. You will often be able to reach all of them in minutes . . . but you won't need to leave your office.

Now read your corrected version aloud.

❸ ▣ Say what will happen in the year 2010.

Examples: *One*
We'll watch more television.
Two
We won't read newspapers.

1 watch more television
2 not read newspapers
3 stay at home more
4 not use the car as much
5 pay all our bills by credit card
6 not visit the bank at all

❹ Join the pairs of sentences in exercise 3. Use *so*.

Example: We'll watch more television
so we won't read
newspapers.

▣ Listen and check.

❺ ▣ Answer the questions and give your own opinions.

Example: *Do you think there will be any newspapers in 2010?*
No, I don't think there will.
or Yes, I think there will.

1 Do you think there will be any newspapers in 2010?
2 And will we send letters?
3 Will we still use credit cards?
4 Will we need passports?
5 Will there still be concerts?
6 Will we still use pens?

PRONUNCIATION GUIDE

In this book a guide is given to the pronunciation of English words using the International Phonetic Alphabet. Word stress is shown by underlining, e.g teacher /tiːtʃə/. In certain dictionaries the mark (') is used to show stress and some different phonetic symbols are used, eg /spɛl/.

/ɑː/	parking /pɑːkɪŋ/ ask /ɑːsk/
/æ/	bank /bæŋk/ jazz /dʒæz/
/aɪ/	five /faɪv/ right /raɪt/
/aɪə/	fire /faɪə/ tired /taɪəd/
/aʊ/	town /taʊn/ how /haʊ/
/aʊə/	our /aʊə/ shower /ʃaʊə/
/ɛ/	ten /tɛn/ spell /spɛl/
/eɪ/	name /neɪm/ eight /eɪt/
/ɛə/	there /ðɛə/ where /wɛə/
/ɪ/	drink /drɪŋk/ live /lɪv/
/i/	happy /hæpi/ twenty /twɛnti/
/iː/	me /miː/ three /θriː/
/ɪə/	near /nɪə/ here /hɪə/
/ɒ/	what /wɒt/ not /nɒt/
/əʊ/	no /nəʊ/ hello /hələʊ/
/ɔː/	four /fɔː/ sport /spɔːt/
/ɔɪ/	boy /bɔɪ/ oil /ɔɪl/
/ʊ/	good /gʊd/ book /bʊk/
/uː/	you /juː/ two /tuː/
/ʊə/	sure /ʃʊə/
/ɜː/	turn /tɜːn/ first /fɜːst/
/ʌ/	one /wʌn/ but /bʌt/
/ə/	teacher /tiːtʃə/ about /əbaʊt/
/b/	bank /bæŋk/ Britain /brɪtən/
/d/	do /duː/ dollar /dɒlə/
/f/	five /faɪv/ fair /fɛə/
/g/	good /gʊd/ Greece /griːs/
/h/	he /hiː/ hat /hæt/
/j/	young /jʌŋ/ yellow /jɛləʊ/
/k/	cook /kʊk/ kilo /kiːləʊ/
/l/	like /laɪk/ love /lʌv/
/m/	my /maɪ/ make /meɪk/
/n/	nine /naɪn/ know /nəʊ/
/p/	pop /pɒp/ pay /peɪ/
/r/	rock /rɒk/ run /rʌn/
/s/	say /seɪ/ spell /spɛl/
/t/	two /tuː/ ten /tɛn/
/v/	verb /vɜːb/ violin /vaɪəlɪn/
/w/	well /wɛl/ water /wɔːtə/
/x/	loch /lɒx/
/z/	zoo /zuː/
/ʃ/	shop /ʃɒp/ she /ʃiː/
/ʒ/	measure /mɛʒə/ leisure /lɛʒə/
/ŋ/	think /θɪŋk/ English /ɪŋglɪʃ/
/tʃ/	cheap /tʃiːp/ cheque /tʃɛk/
/θ/	three /θriː/ think /θɪŋk/
/ð/	then /ðɛn/ with /wɪð/
/dʒ/	jazz /dʒæz/ judo /dʒuːdəʊ/

IRREGULAR VERBS

These irregular verbs appear in this book.

Infinitive	Past simple	Infinitive	Past simple
be	was/were	let	let
become	became	make	made
begin	began	mean	meant
break	broke	meet	met
bring	brought	pay	paid
broadcast	broadcast	put	put
build	built	read	read
buy	bought	/riːd/	/rɛd/
catch	caught	ring	rang
choose	chose	run	ran
come	came	say	said
cost	cost	see	saw
cut	cut	sell	sold
do	did	send	sent
draw	drew	shake	shook
drink	drank	shoot	shot
drive	drove	shut	shut
eat	ate	sing	sang
feel	felt	sit	sat
find	found	speak	spoke
fly	flew	spell	spelled/
forget	forgot		spelt
forgive	forgave	spend	spent
get	got	stand	stood
give	gave	swim	swam
go	went	take	took
have	had	teach	taught
hear	heard	tell	told
hit	hit	think	thought
hurt	hurt	throw	threw
know	knew	under-	under-
learn	learned/	stand	stood
	learnt	wear	wore
leave	left	write	wrote
lend	lent		

Instructions for Student A

UNIT 2   *Lesson 8*   *Activity 7*

Look at the business cards and find out who the people in WHO'S WHO? are.

Greg Murphy	Mary Tyler
Civil Engineer	Civil Engineer
GREENCO Plc	**GREENCO Plc**
156 Wee Nam Road	156 Wee Nam Road
0820 Singapore	0820 Singapore
Tel: (065) 987 654	Tel: (065) 987 654

WPC Holly West
Thames Valley Police HQ
Oxford Road
Kidlington
Oxford OX5 2NX
Tel: (08675) 4343

Henry Green
Personal Assistant to the Managing Director
Mobil Oil Inc
Feldstrasse 38b
8006 Zurich
Switzerland
Tel: (01) 467 589

Now tell Student B who the people in WHO'S WHO? are.

This is Holly West and this is . . .

UNIT 2   *Lesson 9*   *Activity 3*

Don't look at the photo on page 26. Tell Student B if these items are in the photo.

apples   newspaper   orange juice   dress
toothpaste   sugar   train tickets   tomatoes
coffee   bread   postcards   cigarettes   ice-cream
wine   bag

Now look at the photo and listen to Student B. Say if he/she is right.

UNIT 2   *Lesson 10*   *Activity 5*

Complete the chart on page 28 for Rosa.

Rosa is a student in Sevilla. 'I get up at a quarter to eight. I have breakfast at a quarter past eight. I start school at nine and finish at two. I come home from school at half past two. I have lunch at three and I have dinner at nine o'clock. I go to bed at half past ten.'

UNIT 3   *Review*   *Activity 9*

Read the passage below and decide where these sentences go.

a The Brazilians play football everywhere.
b During Carnival time there is samba music day and night, and the streets become huge outdoor dance floors.
c The *praia*, or beach, is the favourite place for people to spend their free time.

Free time in Brazil

Television is very popular in Brazil, but the hot weather makes city apartments uncomfortable and most leisure activities take place outdoors. Most Brazilians live on or near the coast. 1 . . .

Football is the most popular sport and Brazilians take it very seriously. Since the World Cup started, Brazil has reached the final stages every time and has won the championship three times, in 1958, 1962 and 1970. 2 . . . They play on the beach, in the streets, and anywhere there is room to kick a ball around.

Brazilians are famous for their love of singing and dancing, and samba is the national music. 3 . . .

Write down five things which Brazilians like doing in their free time.

Now ask Student B what people in Sweden like doing in their free time.

Do they like watching television? ·

UNIT 4   *Lesson 20*   *Activity 7*

Find the answers to these questions in the article on page 64.

– When was Bob Geldof born?
– When did Band Aid record *Do they know it's Christmas?*
– When did he start to plan the concert in London?
– When did the Philadelphia concert start?

Now work with Student B. Put the events of Bob Geldof's life in the right order.

A Bob Geldof was born on 5 October 1954.
B He started a rock band in . . .

UNIT 5   *Lesson 23*   *Activity 10*

You are the director of the film studio MJM. You are looking for an actor and an actress to play Montana Jones and Candy Barr in the adventure film *The Treasure of Tiger Hill*.

Here are the photographs of MJM's leading actors and actresses.

Mary Robinson   James Tate   Kathy Lynham Peter Steinhof

But they are not suitable for *The Treasure of Tiger Hill*. Decide what the leading actor and actress of the film should look like.

Now ask the directors of Universal Artists and Wiener Brothers to help you.

A Can you help me? I'm looking for an actor to play Montana Jones in the adventure film *The Treasure of Tiger Hill*.

B What about . . .?

A What does he look like?

UNIT 5   *Lesson 24*   *Activity 6*

Read and find out:
– the age when pupils take the first public exam
– the percentage of pupils who go to university
– the percentage of pupils who go to private schools

● There are nearly 28,000 schools in Britain, of which less than 10% are independent or 'private' schools. There are about 515,000 full-time pupils in private education, which is 7% of the total number attending school.

● At the age of 13 to 14, most children have to choose which subjects to take for the GCSE (General Certificate of Secondary Education). This is the first public exam in Britain which most pupils take when they are 16.

● There are 47 state-run universities in Britain, which offer first degree courses lasting three or four years. Only about 5% of school leavers go on to university, usually at the age of 18 or 19.

Now answer questions 5–7 in the chart on page 80.

UNIT 6   *Lesson 26*   *Activity 10*

Act out two conversations.

1 You are in a restaurant and the service is very slow. You wait an hour for your meal. When the bill arrives the waiter has added a service charge. You decide not to pay it.

2 You are on a plane. You paid for a first class ticket, but there was a mistake and there were not enough seats. You want to smoke because you are nervous about flying.

UNIT 6   *Lesson 27*   *Activity 11*

Read this description of your role.

You like football and music and there's a concert by the Stranglers at the Astoria on Saturday evening. You usually stay in bed a long time on Sunday morning, but you like cooking Sunday lunch for your friends. You like reading the newspapers in the evening. You don't really like walking.

Now turn back to page 95 and work with Student B and Student C.

UNIT 6   *Lesson 28*   *Activity 7*

Explain these situations to Student B and ask for information.

How long will it take to get from . . . to . . .?

1 You are a politician. You are leaving London at 8 a.m. on the Brussels express for a midday meeting at the European Commission. You want to know when you will get to the centre of Brussels.

2 You are driving to Spain with your family for a holiday. You are at the Eurotunnel Terminal near Folkestone in England at 9.15 a.m. You want to know how long it will take to get to the French motorway.

3 It's 6 p.m. in Birmingham. You are sending 200 new cars to Frankfurt in Germany. You want to know when the cars will get to Frankfurt.

Now listen and tell Student B what he/she wants to know. Use the information below.

Allow one hour for changing trains in London.	
London–Cardiff	1 hr 43 min
London–Edinburgh	4 hr 37 min
London–Nice	11 hrs
London–Basle	8 hrs
London–Amsterdam	5 hr 30 min

Instructions for Student B

UNIT 2   Lesson 8   Activity 7

Look at the business cards and find out who the people in WHO'S WHO? are.

Kenneth Hill **The Grange Medical Centre** *26 Piedmont Road E6* *Nashville Tennessee* *37500 United States of America* *Tel: (0615) 678 6993*	Mrs Joan Perry *Manager* **National Midland Bank Plc** 357 South High Road Manchester M6 7UD Tel: (061) 564 8255
Dr Anna Biron Dame Edna Memorial Hospital *16/236 Pacific Highway* *Melbourne* *Australia* *Tel: (03) 23956*	**Dr Rodney Jones** Dame Edna Memorial Hospital *16/236 Pacific Highway* *Melbourne* *Australia* *Tel: (03) 23956*

Now tell Student A who the people in WHO'S WHO? are.

This is Anna Biron and this is . . .

UNIT 2   Lesson 9   Activity 3

Look at the photo on page 26 and listen to Student A. Say if he/she is right.

Now tell Student A if these items are in the photo. Don't look at the photo.

shoes   butter   guide book   sun cream   grapes
T-shirt   cheese   map   biscuits   magazine
soap   hotel bill   restaurant bill   water   stamps

UNIT 2   Lesson 10   Activity 5

Complete the chart on page 28 for Dean.

Dean is a rock musician in Vancouver. 'I get up at around half past ten. I don't have breakfast, lunch is about twelve thirty. Then I work late. I start at eight o'clock in the evening and have dinner at around eleven o'clock. I go to bed at three o'clock in the morning.'

UNIT 3   Review   Activity 9

Read the passage below and decide where these sentences go.

a In winter they play ice hockey.
b After work many people relax with a newspaper or magazine.
c Another favourite evening pastime is entertaining at home.

Free time in Sweden

Swedes have plenty of free time because the hours of work are short and holidays are long. 1 . . . The Swedes are among the biggest newspaper readers in the world. Watching television is also a favourite way of relaxing.

Many Swedes go to evening classes to learn a foreign language for their holidays abroad or to practise some handicraft. 2 . . . Most people prefer to meet friends in their own homes, since restaurants are usually very expensive.

The winters are very long in Sweden, so there is plenty of opportunity for winter sports. Skiing is very popular, especially cross-country skiing. The Swedes like football but they only play it in summer. 3 . . . The Swedish national ice hockey team is one of the best in the world.

Write down seven things which Swedes like doing in their free time.

Now ask Student A what people in Brazil like doing in their free time.

Do they like watching television?

UNIT 4   Lesson 20   Activity 7

Find the answers to these questions in the article on page 64.

– When did Bob Geldof start a rock band?
– When did he see the TV news about Ethiopia?
– When did he go to Ethiopia?
– When did the Live Aid concert start?

Now work with Student A. Put the events of Bob Geldof's life in the right order.

A   Bob Geldof was born on . . .
B   He started a rock band in 1975.

UNIT 5   *Lesson 23*   *Activity 10*

You are the director of the film studio Universal Artists. You are looking for an actor and actress to play Luke Spacerider and Princess Starlight in the space film *Beyond the Moons of Jupiter*.

Here are the photographs of Universal Artists' leading actors and actresses.

Rick Armstrong   Sally Williams   Gary Grayson   Anne Dubois

But they are not suitable for *Beyond the Moons of Jupiter*. Decide what the leading actor and actress of the film should look like.

Now ask the directors of MJM and Wiener Brothers to help you.

B   Can you help me? I'm looking for an actress to play Princess Starlight in the space film *Beyond the Moons of Jupiter*.
C   What about . . . ?
B   What does she look like?

UNIT 5   *Lesson 24*   *Activity 6*

Read and find out:
– the age when pupils take the second public exam
– the percentage of pupils who leave at sixteen
– the number of weeks' holiday in a year

● The British school year begins in September and ends in July. There are three terms, with about two weeks' holiday at Christmas, two weeks at Easter, and six weeks in the summer. There are also half-term holidays of about a week in the middle of each term.
● The second public exam in Britain is A (Advanced) level, which is a necessary step for students who want to go to university. Most students take A levels in two or three subjects at the age of 18.
● Children start school at the age of 5, and must stay at school until they are 16. The majority leave school to find work, but about 25% stay on for the sixth form, where they can study for A levels.

Now answer questions 8–10 in the chart on page 80.

UNIT 6   *Lesson 26*   *Activity 10*

Act out two conversations.

1   You are a waiter in a restaurant. You have no one to help you serve thirty customers today. One customer refuses to leave you a service charge, which is a large part of your salary. What do you say?
2   You are in the no-smoking section of a plane. The person beside you lights a cigarette. What do you say?

UNIT 6   *Lesson 27*   *Activity 11*

Read this description of your role.

You like sport and there's a football match on Saturday afternoon. You want to see a Fellini film on television in the evening. On Sunday morning you like to go for a run in the country and then relax in the afternoon. You prefer to eat in the evening and love going to restaurants.

Now turn back to page 95 and work with Student A and Student C.

UNIT 6   *Lesson 28*   *Activity 7*

Listen and tell Student A what he/she wants to know. Use the information below.

Allow one hour for changing trains in London.	
London–Birmingham	1 hr 27 min
London–Brussels	2 hr 45 min
London–Frankfurt	8 hrs
The journey from the Eurotunnel Terminal at Folkestone to the French motorway via the Channel tunnel takes about 1 hr 15 min.	

Now explain these situations to Student A and ask for information.

How long will it take to get from . . . to . . . ?

1   You make computers in Cardiff, Wales. It is 5 a.m. A customer in Amsterdam wants six computers before the end of the working day. You want to know how long it will take your computers to get to Amsterdam.
2   You are on your honeymoon. You are leaving London at midday on an international express. You are looking forward to a champagne lunch before you reach Paris. You want to know if you will be in Nice in time for dinner.
3   You are a student. You are returning from Switzerland on the overnight sleeper which leaves Basle at 10 p.m. . You want to know when you will be back in Edinburgh.

Instructions for Student C

UNIT 5   *Lesson 23*   *Activity 10*

You are the director of the film studio Wiener Brothers. You are looking for an actor and an actress to play Philip Bogart and Laura Lamont in the detective film *Lonely Streets*.

Here are the photographs of Wiener Brothers' leading actors and actresses.

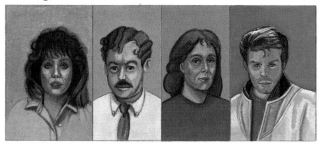

Lucia Fantoni   Max Mildner   Jane Morgen   Terry O'Sullivan

But they are not suitable for *Lonely Streets*. Decide what the leading actor and actress of the film should look like.

Now ask the directors of MJM and Universal Artists to help you.

C Can you help me? I'm looking for an actor to play Philip Bogart in the detective film *Lonely Streets*.
A What about . . . ?
C What does he look like?

UNIT 6   *Lesson 27*   *Activity 11*

Read this description of your role.

You like music but you don't like going to concerts very much. There's a concert on the radio on Saturday evening. You usually go for a long walk in the country on Sundays and have lunch in a pub. You prefer to do very little in the evening.

Now turn back to page 95 and work with Student A and Student B.

Instructions for all students

UNIT 5   *Lesson 23*   *Activity 8*

Write out the description word for word. Don't turn back to read it again. It doesn't matter if you can't remember every word. Ask other students for help.

UNIT 5   *Review*   *Activity 3*

Use your list of stressed words to write out the report word for word. Don't turn back to read it again. Ask other students for help.

UNIT 5   *Review*   *Activity 11*

Complete the notes below without looking back at the profile on page 84.

Name	Adragon Eastwood Demello
Age	. . . .
Nationality	. . . .
Education	Cabrillo College, California
Achievements:	
. . . .	Said first word
2½ years	Good at . . . . and geometry
4 years	Learning . . . . , ... and philosophy
. . . .	Wrote computer programs, built a robot, went to college
Now	. . . . expert, writes . . . . Writing a novel
Ambition	Father wants him to . . . .

Then check your notes with another student. Ask and answer questions.

How old was he when he went to college?

UNIT 6   *Lesson 26*   *Activity 8*

Use your list of words and phrases to write out the letter word for word. Don't turn back to read it again. Ask other students for help.

UNIT 6   *Review*   *Activity 9*

Write down as many items as you can remember. Don't look back at the picture on page 103 until your teacher tells you!